UNDERSTANDING
SOCIALISM

UNDERSTANDING
SOCIALISM

Richard D. Wolff

Edited by Liz Phillips & Maria Carnemolla

Published by Democracy at Work
PO Box 30941
New York, NY 10011
info@democracyatwork.info
www.democracyatwork.info

ISBN: 978-0-578-22734-4

Available through Lulu.com

Cover design by Luis de la Cruz

Other Books from Democracy at Work:
Understanding Marxism by Richard D. Wolff

Coming in 2020...
Capire Il Marxismo di Richard D. Wolff, the Italian translation of
Understanding Marxism

Acknowledgements

The editors would like to thank Richard D. Wolff for his incredibly generous contribution in writing this book. The proceeds from the sales will support Democracy at Work, a non-profit that he founded in 2012. The organization's mission is to create media that analyzes capitalism critically as a systemic problem and advocates for democratizing workplaces as part of a systemic solution.

Professor Wolff and the editors would like to acknowledge the hard work of the following dedicated volunteers who offered their time and skills to the copy-editing of this book. Their attentiveness, dedication, and insights polished and deepened its contents.

Marilou Baughman
Gloria Denton
Andrea Iannone
Jake Keyel
Christian Lewis
Steven Payne

Democracy at Work would also like to thank artist Luis de la Cruz, whose work graces the cover, and who is always a delight to work with.

Contents

Introduction

Socialism is a kind of yearning for a better life than what capitalism permits for most people. Socialist yearnings are as old as capitalism itself, because they are its products. Where and when capitalism's problems and failings have accumulated criticism and critics, socialist voices have risen. And so it is again now.

Any serious discussion of socialism must begin by acknowledging socialism's rich diversity. Whatever particular aspects of socialism we choose to analyze, they need to be located within socialism's complexity. That avoids presenting one's own interpretation as if it were the entirety of socialism. In this book, I focus on the economic aspects of socialism, how it differs from capitalism in broad outlines. I am more interested in socialist critiques of capitalism and their implications about socialist alternatives than in the particulars of the few, early experiments in erecting socialist systems (USSR, People's Republic of China, and so on) that history so far offers. Finally, my own education and work constrain me to concentrate on Western Europe and North America. Some important aspects of socialism are thus not covered or discussed here.

Yearnings for better lives, such as socialism proposes, are not new. In slave societies, the slaves hoped and dreamed of lives less hard and less out of their own control. Their yearning aimed to obtain freedom. They sought social change that would preclude any one person being the property of another.

In feudal societies, the serfs — "free" in the sense that no one "owned" them — yearned for better lives too. Their subordination to lords included heavy labor and other burdens that they wanted lifted. They hoped and dreamed of a society in which they would not be bound to the land, the lord of that land, and the feudal dues of labor and subservience. The serfs mobilized in the 1789 French Revolution to demand liberty, equality, and brotherhood. In effect, the serfs had expanded on what the slaves had called freedom.

In the American Revolution against British King George III, the revolutionaries were neither slaves nor serfs. They were mostly self-employed farmers, craftspeople, and merchants subject to a foreign feudal kingdom. Their yearnings thus differed from those of slaves and serfs. They wanted liberty as individuals to pursue their dreams without hindrance from feudalism or monarchism, whether foreign or domestic. They added democracy to the goals advanced by the slaves and serfs before them.

The different systems of slavery, feudalism, and small-scale self-employment produced masses of people yearning for better lives. Eventually, each of those systems provoked revolutions. Many people then sought to break away from and go beyond those systems. The French and American revolutions marked key moments in the social transformations of major pre-capitalist systems into capitalist ones.

By "capitalist system" we mean that particular organization of production in which the basic human relation is employer/employee instead of master/slave, lord/serf, or individual self-employment. The revolutionaries who wanted and built capitalism hoped and believed that transitions to employer/employee relations of production would bring with them the liberty, equality, brotherhood, and democracy they yearned for. The revolutions' leaders promised — to themselves and to the people they led — that those goals would be achieved.

But the transitions to capitalist employer/employee relations that increasingly replaced the previous slave, feudal, and self-employment relations of production had unintended consequences. Capitalism soon proved to be different from what its revolutionaries had hoped. While it enabled some people to be more free and more independent than slaves, serfs, or self-employed subjects of monarchies had been, it also seriously limited freedom, independence, and democracy for many. Capitalism betrayed many of the promises made by its advocates. It produced and reproduced great inequalities of income and wealth. Poverty proved to be endemic, as capitalism seemed equally adept at producing and

3

reproducing both wealth and poverty. The capitalist rich used their wealth to shape and control politics and culture. Democratic forms hid very undemocratic content. The cyclical instability attending capitalism constantly threatened and hurt large numbers, and so on.

Growing numbers of employees within capitalism began to yearn for better lives. They defined those yearnings first in the familiar terms of the earlier French and American revolutions: equality, fraternity, liberty, and democracy. They criticized a capitalism that failed to deliver those to most people and demanded social changes to achieve them. Many people still continue to want a better, softer, friendlier capitalism, where government regulates and intervenes to achieve more of what the French and American revolutionaries had yearned for and promised. They often self-define as "socialists."

However, capitalism's development provoked another, different perspective that also called itself socialism. In that view, capitalism had not broken from slavery, feudalism, and monarchy nearly as much as its advocates had imagined. Slavery had masters/slaves, feudalism had lords/serfs, and monarchy had kings/subjects as key sources of their inequalities, lack of freedom, oppressions, and conflicts. The employer/employee relation of production in capitalism generated parallel problems.

Capitalism installed monarchies inside individual workplaces, even as monarchies outside workplaces were rejected. Kings mostly disappeared, but inside each workplace the owners or their designated boards of directors assumed king-like powers.

Capitalism proclaimed democracy outside workplaces, where people resided, but banned it from inside its workplaces.

For some, socialism protests against all the dichotomies: slave/master, serf/lord, subject/king, and employee/employer. It seeks their abolition in favor of democratically self-governing communities of equals. Such socialists insist that democracy applies to the economy as well as to politics. They see no way for politics to be genuinely democratic if it rests on a non-democratic economic basis. The corruption common to all political systems resting on capitalist economies — endlessly experienced, regularly exposed, and constantly reproduced — is their proof. The inequalities attending all capitalist economies are protected, and thus reproduced, because even a formally democratic politics disproportionately empowers capitalism's employer class.

How to concretely organize socialism, and how to achieve transition to it from capitalism, have always been issues of disagreement and debate among socialists. Anyone referring to *the* socialist position on what constitutes a socialist economy and society, or on how to achieve transition, is making a major mistake. Socialism is more like a tradition of multiple different streams of thought about these questions. The extraordinarily rapid spread of socialism across the globe over the last century and a half brought it to societies with very different histories, economic development, cultures, and so on. Many different interpretations of socialism emerged. Likewise, practical socialist movements over the same period display successes and failures — in labor struggles, party politics, and in early efforts to construct socialist economies and societies — that also shaped diverse kinds of socialism.

The debates among socialists have sometimes been extreme. Some interpretations view others as outside the tradition, not "real" or "true" socialism. Some interpretations added adjectives to "socialism" to distinguish among the interpretations. Examples include "democratic," "market," "libertarian," "anarcho-," "eco-," "evolutionary," "revolutionary," "Soviet," "Christian," "utopian," "scientific," "national," "parliamentary," "state," "Stalinist," and more. Socialists *never* universally accepted or recognized any one authority's definition of socialism. Instead, socialism has always been a tradition of multiple, different, contested streams of thought and practice. We try here to explain when and why we use one or some among socialism's interpretations and when we discuss the tradition as a whole.

In the name of socialism, individuals, groups, movements, parties, and governments have sometimes acted in ways that other socialists and non-socialists have found unjustified or even horrific. While the same indictment applies to Christianity, or democracy, or freedom, etc., that is not an excuse. Stalin and Pol Pot are stains on the history of socialism that it must account for and reject. The Spanish Inquisition, missionaries' misdeeds, holy wars against infidels, and countless wars among different interpretations are parallel stains on Christianity. Centuries of colonialism, the slave trade, world war, and mass poverty in the midst of great wealth stain capitalism.

Transition from capitalism to one or another kind of socialism does not guarantee that all socialist goals will be achieved or that none will be abused. The abolition of slavery did not mean freedom was achieved and never subsequently abused.

6

Likewise, the end of serfdom by a revolutionary transition to capitalism did not guarantee liberty, equality, and fraternity for all. Nonetheless, the passing of slavery and of feudalism were important, necessary, positive steps for humanity. Socialists argue the same for the transition from capitalism to socialism. Indeed, socialists today, across nearly all their different streams and interpretations, recognize that the tradition benefits as much from acknowledging abusive usages of socialism (not to be repeated) as from celebrating and building successful usages.

Socialism is continually reborn, since the problems of capitalism, especially inequality and cyclical instability, remain unsolved. A particular burden for today's new generation of socialists — and for the writing of this book — arises from the last half century's taboo on socialism, especially in the United States. That taboo left a legacy of ignorance about socialism in general and about its many profound changes over the last 50 years. My hope is that this book helps to overcome that taboo and its legacy, and thereby helps build a new socialism.

Chapter I

A Brief History: How Socialism Got to its Here and Now

Socialism grew from a small European social movement two centuries ago into a huge global movement today. Historically, that is far faster than comparable movements in history, such as Rome's empire, Christianity, or Islam. Even the capitalism that spawned socialism as its critical "other" began earlier and so grew less quickly. Today's socialism reflects its rapid spread across a changing world's diverse natural, political, economic, and cultural conditions. A brief look at socialism's remarkable history offers us a useful angle for understanding it.

Socialism exploded in 19th-century Europe and took off across the continent. Echoes and ramifications of the French and American revolutions provoked correspondingly revolutionary thinking and writing. In philosophy, politics, economics (then called "political economy"), and culture, many ruptures and breakthroughs occurred. The remaining feudalism and feudal empires disintegrated, and industrial capitalism and ethnic nationalisms spread. The 1848 Revolutions led to major reorganizations of Europe's map (especially the unifications of Germany and Italy), and capitalist colonialism took major steps toward creating an integrated world economy. All such events spurred the development and expansion of socialism as well.

Socialism gathered the critics and criticisms of capitalism's evident tendencies to widen income and wealth differences. Socialism came to stand for a yearning toward far greater equality. Socialism likewise accumulated the protests and protesters against capitalism's instability, its built-in cycles that confronted the working class with sudden unemployment and income loss, on average every four to seven years. The plague of recession and depression feared by most employers and employees alike struck many as an utterly irrational feature of capitalism and more than sufficient to provoke a yearning for a system that would not need or permit such cycles.

By the second half of the 19th century, European socialists were numerous and self-confident enough to form social movements, labor unions, and political parties. Socialist newspapers, books, and pamphlets spread their ideas. Serious theoreticians (especially Marx, Engels, and their students) added depth and reach to socialism, developing the tradition into a substantive literature of social criticism, analysis, and proposals for making social change. Marx's *Capital, Volume 1* defined a fundamental injustice — exploitation — located in capitalism's core employer/employee relationship.

Exploitation, in Marx's terms, describes the situation in which employees produce more value for employers than the value of wages paid to them. Capitalist exploitation, Marx showed, shaped everything else in capitalist societies. Yearning for a better society, socialists increasingly included demands for the end of exploitation, replacing the employer/employee relationship with an alternative production organization in which employees functioned democratically as their own employer.

In 1871, socialists seized power in Paris and established and governed a commune there. For a few weeks, Europe and the world glimpsed some outlines of how society would function differently were socialism to replace capitalism. Socialists also glimpsed a basic strategy for transition from capitalism to socialism. Socialists would capture state power and use it to create, protect, and develop the socialist alternative to capitalism.

Socialists in 19th-century Europe generally embraced the key slogans of the French and American revolutions: liberty, equality, fraternity, and democracy. What distressed and activated them was that actually existing capitalisms had failed to achieve those ideals. Socialism was the demand to go further, to be more "progressive," precisely to realize liberty, equality, fraternity, and democracy. If capitalism could or would not move forward in that way, then it needed to be pushed aside for a better system, namely socialism.

Several central issues took form as major alternative streams of socialist thought coalesced around them. One issue concerned building socialism around images, sketches, and even functioning models of the desired post-capitalist society. Cooperative workplaces, collectivist communities, anti-individualist kinship groups, and more comprised social models that inspired "utopian" socialists. Examples include Robert Owen and his New Lanark community, Charles Fourier and his Phalanstery, Etienne Cabet and his worker cooperatives, and many others. The utopians often believed that to achieve progress beyond the capitalisms of their day, people living within those systems had to see and experience today anticipations of future socialism. Constructing and promoting such anticipations became a major strategy to win adherents for a transition from capitalism to socialism.

Other socialists tilted their emphases elsewhere. Marx and Engels offered a "scientific" socialism as a critique of utopian socialism. They argued that beautiful utopias would not produce revolutions against capitalism nor transitions to socialism. Rather, transformation would emerge when the tensions, conflicts, and crises resulting from capitalism's internal contradictions produced the desire and capacity for social change among a part of the population that could achieve that change. For Marx and Engels, the potential revolutionary agent was the industrial proletariat — the working class — allied with those intellectuals who understood the future dangers inherent in capitalism's internal contradictions. Socialists to this day debate the roles of utopian impulses and models on the one hand, and the mobilization of a revolutionary working class inside capitalism on the other, in relation to strategies of transitioning to and sustaining socialism.

Another major issue agitating and dividing socialists, particularly in the latter half of the 19th century in Europe, was the debate over reform versus revolution. Would the transition occur and best be furthered by accumulated reforms of capitalism, or would a sharp break by means of revolution be required? Eventually labeled as the debate between "evolutionary" and "revolutionary" socialisms, its object was to determine the best strategy for the socialist political parties then emerging. One side, often associated with the German socialist Eduard Bernstein, prioritized "parliamentary socialism." They believed that socialists should contest in elections and engage electoral coalitions around reforms of capitalism, yet simultaneously argue and push always for the further social transformation needed to secure a new, better society. Such a strategy could build the mass consciousness and the political-party apparatus to take state power. With such a political base organized by a mass party, acquiring state power would enable a transition from capitalism to socialism that capitalists and their supporters could not block.

Against such a strategy, "revolutionary" socialists, such as Vladimir Lenin and Rosa Luxemburg, countered that capitalists would never relinquish their wealth and power without resorting to extreme measures, including mass violence. In the revolutionaries' view, it was naïve and foolish not to anticipate and prepare for those reactions to socialist advances. Such socialists argued that it was always appropriate to analyze the internal contradictions and tensions within capitalism to identify moments when revolutionary ruptures were possible. Just as the English, American, and French revolutions were key events in the European transition beyond feudalism to capitalism, such socialists anticipated parallel revolutions for the transition from capitalism to socialism. Debaters of the most effective path toward socialism sometimes also proclaimed middle grounds: commitments to struggle for reforms but always with an explicit caveat that reforms would never be secure until a basic change to socialism had been accomplished, which required a revolutionary break.

Just as socialists have long debated the relative importance of utopian versus scientific socialisms, and reformist versus revolutionary socialisms, the 20th century brought forward a new and different kind of debate. The Soviet revolution of 1917 inaugurated the first enduring government committed to socialism: the Union of Soviet Socialist Republics (USSR). The 1917 revolutionaries (especially Lenin) drew many important lessons from the very short-lived French socialist experiments in the Paris Commune of 1871. Marx's analysis of why the Paris Commune survived so briefly served Lenin with significant guides that helped the Soviet revolution become the first durable experiment in constructing a socialist government.

From its beginning, the USSR provoked debate among socialists. Disputes focused on whether Soviet leaders' decisions properly applied pre-1917 socialist ideas and principles. On a deeper level, the European socialist movement had to confront two significant changes from what had agitated and driven socialism during the 19th century.

First, socialism now had two different contexts that became two distinct, albeit also connected, social projects. Socialists living and working inside still-capitalist countries continued to focus on how to mobilize workers for transformation to socialism. Socialists living and working in the USSR, meanwhile, focused on constructing, protecting, and strengthening a socialist economy, society, and government. Many of the latter socialists appealed to their comrades inside capitalist countries to give priority to defending and supporting socialism's "first country," the USSR.

On that question socialists split everywhere. Socialists supporting the Soviet interpretation mostly changed their name to "communists" and broke away to form communist parties. Socialists who were more or less skeptical or critical of Soviet actions and statements generally held on to the name "socialist." Debates swirled openly among multiple socialist and communist parties, and also (usually less openly) within them, over whether and how the USSR embodied, distorted, or betrayed socialism. Those debates continued even after the USSR imploded in 1989.

The new USSR's charismatic leader, Lenin, took the position that what the 1917 revolution had accomplished was what he called "state capitalism." By that he meant that socialists had achieved and sustained state power and used it to displace private capitalists from their enterprise positions. The new USSR nationalized industry and placed state functionaries in the place formerly occupied by private capitalist boards of directors. The employer/employee structure of capitalism had been retained, but *who the employers were* had been changed. Debates among socialists had to broaden to consider state capitalism alongside private capitalism and socialism as forms relevant to socialist strategy. However, that broadening lasted only a short time. Lenin's death in 1924, the bitter split within the Soviet leadership between Leon Trotsky and Josef Stalin, and Stalin's emergence as the dominant leader starkly changed socialist debates.

Perhaps Stalin's most consequential early decision was to declare that the USSR had achieved socialism. What Lenin had called "state capitalism" thus became "socialism." Stalin offered the USSR as the successfully achieved transition from capitalism to socialism, the model for those seeking socialism everywhere. Whatever Stalin's intent — perhaps to give the long-suffering Soviet people a sense that all their sacrifices had achieved their goal — his declaration had deeply problematic effects. It identified socialism — for the world — with a social system at once poor, wracked with internal conflicts, and tightly controlled by a harsh political dictatorship. Socialism's enemies have used this identification ever since to equate political dictatorship with socialism. Of course, this required obscuring or denying that (1) dictatorships have often existed in capitalist societies and (2) socialisms have often existed without dictatorships. That obscuring and denying continues to this day.

The second big change that the first half of the 20th century brought into socialism came from the rise of local movements against capitalist imperialism. Their targets were Europe's formal colonialism, chiefly in Asia and Africa, and the US's less formal, but no less real, colonialism in Latin America. Those oppositional movements increasingly found their way to socialism. Sometimes, students attending universities in colonizing countries encountered socialists and socialism there. More generally, colonized people seeking independence took inspiration from, and saw alliance possibilities with, workers fighting exploitation in the colonizing countries. The latter increasingly glimpsed similar possibilities from the other side.

Socialism spread, via capitalist imperialism, to all colonies and thereby helped to create a global socialist tradition. The multiple interpretations of socialism that had evolved in capitalism's centers thus spawned yet more and further-differentiated interpretations of socialism. In particular, diverse streams within the anti-colonial and anti-imperialist tradition — theoretical and practical — interacted with and enriched socialism.

Over the second half of the 20th century, until 1989, global socialism exhibited both its greatest successes and worst setbacks. By the 1970s, the USSR had recovered from World War II to become the world's second superpower. Communist parties held power in Eastern Europe, China, Cuba, Vietnam, and beyond. Anti-colonial movements were often infused with socialist ideas and led by socialists. The Vietnam War pitted one product of the anti-colonial-cum-socialist movement against its opposite. The final defeat of the US in Vietnam in 1975 marked a kind of peak for modern socialism.

Socialist parties frequently formed governments, alone or in coalitions (sometimes with communist parties), across Europe after 1945. The socialism/communism split that developed after 1917 was hardened in and by the Cold War. Socialism — often called "democratic socialism," "social democracy," or "socialist democracy" — took hold in Northern and Western Europe especially. Workplaces there were mostly left in the hands of private capitalists. However, the government sometimes operated some major industries (e.g., utilities, transport, banks) while controlling the economy with heavy regulations and taxation. The government's goals included labor protections, income redistribution, and provision of basic welfare via subsidized education, housing, transport, and health care. This kind of socialism stressed its difference from — and often political opposition to — the communist system in the Eastern European countries allied to the USSR. Those countries also referred to their economic systems as "socialist." In them, the government owned and operated large sections of industry and agriculture, and provided more subsidized public services. Social democrats and communists criticized and debated one another. At the same time, the celebrants of private capitalism mostly attacked both kinds of socialism.

Dissenters criticized both of the major streams, or types, of socialism. For example, some believed that the communist stream empowered the state apparatus excessively, in violation of the bottom-up notion of social power they identified with socialism. Others found social democracy left too much power and wealth concentrated in the hands of large private capitalist interests. Social-democratic regulations and public services were always insecure, always vulnerable to well-financed attacks when private capitalists opposed them. The social democracies' capitalist-generated inequalities rendered their democracies not genuinely socialist in such dissenters' view.

In the United States a peculiarly skewed notion of socialism took hold, especially among those who disliked it, but also among the general public. Large segments of the population came to view the terms "communist," "socialist," "anarchist," "Marxist," and for many also "liberal," as synonyms. They were all "anti-American," and there was really little point or need to distinguish among them. This unusual perspective was partly the fruit of an admittedly poor education system unbalanced by Cold War ideological imperatives. Waves of McCarthyite opposition to communism — as well as left-wing, center-left, and even liberal politics — have swept through the US since the mid-1940s, faded in some parts of the country while remaining strong in others. Such opposition has even resurfaced again now in the Trump era. Those waves effectively destroyed the US communist and socialist parties to an extent rarely equaled elsewhere after World War II. The repressions also taught large portions of the US public to suspect, dismiss, demonize, and avoid all the synonyms equally.

The taboo on socialism imposed by anti-communism in the US after World War II had kept socialism from being taught in most schools. And when it was, teachers treated it dismissively and briefly. They needed to prove their anti-socialist credentials amid a general demonization across social institutions of all things socialist. The 1950s firing of teachers with known socialist sympathies had been an effective warning. US labor unions, too, were caught up in the anti-socialism sentiment and turned against what were often their most militant members and organizers. Thus, unlike its counterparts in most other capitalist countries, organized labor in the US largely severed its previously close connections with socialist organizations and individuals. The 50-year decline of the US labor movement was partly a result of anti-socialist purges inside US unions as they tried to show a loyalty to capitalism that they hoped would protect them. It did not.

✝ For many, communism, socialism, Marxism, anarchism, and more recently terrorism, are all noxious anti-American ideologies and practices that differ only in their spelling. From the mid-1940s until Bernie Sanders' 2016 campaign for president, any candidate accepting the label "socialist" thereby risked political suicide. It was not unusual in the US to see almost all government activity (other than the military) attacked as socialist (e.g., the post office, Amtrak, TVA, Medicare, Medicaid, and so on). Thus, countless Soviet scholars could and did explain that the USSR was socialist — or even state capitalist — and merely hoped one day to develop further into communism. Nonetheless, few in the US paid attention. For most, either word applied synonymously. Such was not the case in Europe, where most people knew from family, neighbors, newspapers, and so on, what rough boundaries separated socialists from communists, etc.

The implosion of the USSR and its Eastern European allies in 1989-1990 set back socialism generally, but especially the communist stream. The social-democracy stream was less affected. However, many of socialism's critics have since portrayed the end of the USSR as some sort of final victory for capitalism in its 20th-century struggle with socialism/communism. Amid the capitalist triumphalism, all strains of socialism were thrown together as having somehow all expired. The reality would soon prove quite different.

Capitalist triumphalism attached itself to the neoliberalism that surged in the 1980-2008 period. Neoliberalism is an ideology holding that deregulated market-exchange and private- (not state-) owned and -operated enterprises always yield superior economic results, including in housing, health care, education, etc. Sustained economic growth (its dependence on debt expansion ignored or downplayed) enabled the idea that a "new economy" had emerged that would grow forever and would finally bury an abandoned socialism. Many socialists and communists were depressed and deactivated by the triumphalism and perceived economic growth, especially in the old centers of capitalism (Western Europe, North America, and Japan).

Yet just below the radar of most Western public opinion, China's brand of socialism — a hybrid state capitalism that included both communist and social-democratic streams — proved it could grow faster over more years than any capitalist economy had ever done. By early in the 21st century, China had become the second economic superpower, after the US, and was gaining fast. Socialism, it turned out, had not died, but it had moved its center east. That should not have surprised anyone, since capitalism had done the same.

The 2008 global crash of capitalism, and the neoliberalism that had preceded it since the 1970s, added new disruptions to the history of socialism. Neoliberalism generated a surge of income and consumption growth that challenged the Soviet and Eastern European socialisms. Those systems had focused on industrial growth (impressively achieved) that prioritized capital goods and infrastructure over individual consumption. The latter was promised but largely postponed to facilitate the growth of the former. But their populations, badly affected by World War II, resisted and resented repetitions of reduced, postponed, or slow consumption growth. Reduced Cold War tensions, plus the spread of television and other displays of disparate consumption levels, plus building resentments over limited civil liberties, combined to collapse the Soviet and Eastern European socialist governments. A relatively peaceful transition away from them began.

Ironically, because little internal debate had been allowed by those governments, the broad citizenry knew little about the diverse streams of socialism. The existing socialist governments had presented their shared interpretation of socialism as the only valid, real version. Thus the only alternative to the socialism that most Eastern Europeans knew was its arch-other, namely Western capitalism. The idea that there were other kinds of socialism than what existed in Eastern Europe — and that their citizens' aspirations might best be achieved via transition to one of them — was rarely put forward. In the rush to exit from Eastern European socialism, the crowds surged toward Western capitalism with but a few, unheeded voices urging that the desired goal be Scandinavia or Germany, not the UK or US. It was another history lesson showing the deep dangers everywhere of shutting down debate over alternative systems.

The economic surge of Western capitalism, despite being debt-driven, created a near euphoric notion of capitalism's ascendancy. That was reinforced into full euphoria with the collapse of the world's first socialist state, the USSR, and its post-World War II European allies. The 20th century's struggle between capitalism and socialism seemed over, won definitively by capitalism. The future would be perpetual capitalist growth benefiting all. Warning signs — including the hard historical fact that capitalism has suffered costly, periodic boom-and-bust cycles across its history — were widely ignored. Both government and corporate debts accumulated, and new populations were introduced to the joys of consumer debts. Many thought it need never end. But it did in 2007 and 2008 when debt bubbles burst and took down the global capitalism system.

Once-proud megabanks and other megacorporations suddenly stopped bashing governments as wasteful, inefficient burdens on the private sector's back. Instead their private jets took them to global capitals where they begged to be bailed out by trillions of dollars or euros of government money. Given the corporations' political power, the governments responded. They financed huge bailouts with massive additional government debts. Once done, governments decided to rein in the exploding debts by imposing austerity — at least slowing, if not reducing, government spending and borrowing. Public employment, pensions, and public services became major targets for cuts.

Given the neoliberal mentality cultivated over the prior decades, most "leaders" foresaw few risks in their austerity policies. Few imagined that many people would balk at the sequential spectacle of (1) megacapitalists profiting from a debt bubble they helped to create, (2) those same capitalists securing a government bailout when that bubble burst, and (3) leaders then imposing austerity on average citizens to offset the bailout. Nor did the leaders see the dangers in demanding that the working classes they had victimized also absorb the social costs of massive new waves of desperate immigrants.

They were wrong. A revolt commenced, slowly at first, differing with national and regional contexts. Capitalism's instability, inequality, and injustice were just too much. Increasingly, voters turned against the traditional old political leaders and parties, the center-left and center-right that had comfortably alternated in power. Both had dutifully administered the neoliberal regimes in North America, Western Europe, and Japan since the 1970s. Both had cooperated in bailing out the collapsed megacorporations from 2008 to 2010. And both had then promised the people to ease austerity but, once in power, mostly did the opposite.

"Populisms" of the left and right surged into political prominence. Some formed new political parties. Some entered strained coalitions with the old center-lefts and center-rights. Some forced alliances in which they subsumed elements of the older, traditional parties under a new "populist" leadership. Sometimes they governed. And sometimes they refused to play parliamentary politics and remained "populist" movements. On the left, such populisms often included explicit anti-capitalist aspects. On the right, flirtations, or more, with fascism often occurred.

Socialism suffered a peculiar combination of decline and rebirth in the aftermath of the 2008 capitalist collapse. It continued the decline that had set in after the 1970s and had accelerated with the demise of the USSR and Eastern European socialist governments. Social-democratic parties began a steady loss of voters and social support, partly because of their accommodations to neoliberalism, especially when that included acceptance of austerity policies. Some socialist parties dissolved. Some entered coalitions with their former adversaries, the traditional center-right parties. All these maneuvers failed to stem the decline of traditional socialism.

But rebirths also occurred. In some European countries, explicitly anti-capitalist parties formed that were socialist in substance but ambivalent about the name. The word "socialism" had acquired a host of bad associations in a century of demonization by its enemies, who often equated socialism with the worst programs undertaken in its name (by Stalin, Pol Pot, etc.). After its global crash in 2008-2010, capitalism's veneer was badly broken and a renewed socialism burst forth. In the US, the Occupy Wall Street movement in 2011 included explicit and self-confident affirmations of both anti-capitalism and pro-socialism convictions in ways not seen in the prior half century of mass social movements. Then Bernie Sanders' breakthrough 2016 campaign, in which he ran for president as an explicit "democratic socialist," returned socialism to a place within major portions of public discourse about US politics and society.

In each country on earth, socialism exists, advances, and retreats. It processes the lessons and bears the scars of its history there. Yet each country and its socialism are also shaped by socialism's global history: by now a richly accumulated tradition of many diverse streams (interpretations, tendencies, etc.). They reflect its two centuries of gains and losses, successes and failures, declines and rebirths, and critical responses to capitalism's shifting fortunes and contradictions. Socialism's repeated revivals, like its global spread, attest to its deep relevance to a troubled capitalist world, past and present. We need to understand socialism because it has shaped, and will continue to shape, us all. It is the greatest assemblage we possess of the thoughts, experiences, and experiments accomplished by those yearning to do better than capitalism.

Chapter II

What Is Socialism?

Socialism is a yearning by people living in a capitalist economic system, whether private or state capitalist, to do better than what that capitalism permits and enables. By "doing better," socialists mean many things. One is having work that is more socially meaningful, less physically and environmentally destructive, and more secure in delivering an adequate income for yourself and your family than what is generally available in capitalist societies. Another is having the lifelong education, leisure, and civil freedoms to pursue real participation in politics, intimate and friendship relationships, and cultural activities of your choice. Socialists want to be able to explore and develop their full potentials as individuals and members of society while contributing to its welfare and growth.

Of course, these are abstractions and generalizations, but they suffice at this early stage of our argument. Socialists believe such desires are generally frustrated for most people in capitalist societies. Transition from a capitalist to a socialist society is then the means to achieve a society that successfully provides all people with better lives in the sense conveyed above.

In societies with a slave economic system, many slaves yearned for emancipation from the horrific burdens and constraints imposed on them. Their thoughts, dreams, and actions eventually contributed to achieving this goal. Likewise, serfs wanted to abolish the burdens imposed on them by the feudal economic system, and over time they helped make the break from that system. Socialists recognize the uniqueness of slavery and feudalism and also draw inspiration from the slaves' and serfs' struggles against these past economic systems. Socialists want to make a parallel break from capitalism.

Slaves and serfs learned that freedom, liberty, and the overcoming of slavery and feudalism did not magically solve all their problems. Socialists have come to learn the same about socialism. Ending slavery and feudalism were enormously important, progressive steps taken in human history. Socialism, too, will not be a panacea, but it will, in socialists' views, represent a major progressive improvement over capitalism.

Beyond their shared yearning, socialists advocate a variety of criticisms of capitalism, a variety of strategies for transition to socialism, and a variety of conceptions of what socialism is.

Because in most cases socialists focus on the economy, so shall we here.

Any economy is a set of ways and means to produce and distribute goods and services that the people in that community need or want. Our food, clothing, shelter, amusements, transport, and much more comprise our needs and wants. Our labor combines with tools and equipment and workplaces, as so many inputs, to produce goods and services, as so many outputs. Before production, resources (such as land, water, space, etc.) need to be distributed to workplaces to be available to the laborers as production inputs. After production, the outputs (goods and services) need to be distributed to those who consume them. An economy comprises the production and distribution of productive resources and production's outputs.

As a way of organizing the production and distribution of a society's goods and services, socialism differs from capitalism and indeed from many other economic systems. In socialism, the whole community of people served by, and living with, or in, an economy participate democratically in producing and distributing goods and services. In slavery, this is clearly not the case. In a slave economy, participants are divided into masters and slaves. Masters control (and literally own) the productive inputs, including the laborers themselves, and decide the fate of slaves in both production and distribution. In feudalism, economic participants are divided into lords and serfs. The latter are not property as in slavery, but they occupy social positions based on the feudal positions of their parents. Children of serfs are likewise usually serfs, and often of the same lord or his children. Children of lords become lords or find associated positions within the feudal economy. Like masters, lords exercise a socially dominant power that derives in large part from their position in relation to production and distribution. Masters and lords are usually few, relative to the numbers of slaves and serfs.

Capitalism is different from slavery, feudalism, and socialism. Capitalism divides participants in production and distribution into employers and employees. Employers are few; employees are many. Employers direct and control employees' work with regard to the production and distribution of goods and services. Employees are not anyone's property, nor are they bound to the land or to the employer of their parents. They are "free" in the sense that they can voluntarily enter into a contract to work for any employer they choose who is hiring employees. Hiring is the purchase of an employee's "labor power" — a person's ability to work over a specific period of time. Labor power is paid for with products or money called a "wage." Wages did not exist in slavery or feudalism, as the relationship of the two primary groups involved in those systems generally secured the work of one for the other without a labor contract.

Another different economic system entails individuals working alone, say as farmers, craftspersons, service providers, etc. In producing and distributing resources and products, such persons work individually. Their economy displays no dichotomy of the sorts encountered in slavery (master/slave), feudalism (lord/serf), or capitalism (employer/employee). Likewise, such an economy is not socialist since it does not entail the democratic and collective decision-making in production and distribution that would occur in a socialist system. Typically called "self-employed" in modern economic terminology, such an economy of individual producers is found throughout much of human history, often occurring alongside and interacting with slave, feudal, capitalist, or socialist systems.

Indeed, it is important here to note that actually existing economies, past and present, often display co-existing economic systems. Thus, the US had capitalism in the North and slavery in the South before the Civil War. Likewise, today capitalist corporations (with boards of directors functioning as employers within them) co-exist and interact with self-employed lawyers, architects, graphic designers, and so on, who are operating within a different, non-capitalist (i.e., non-employer/employee) economic system. In both these examples, there are market-exchange relations between participants in the two different, co-existing economic systems. In other words, while their organizations of production are different — capitalist in the corporation, self-employment in the lawyer's office — they share the same distribution system: namely, market exchange.

Socialism allows such co-existing systems as well. What the USSR called its socialist (i.e., state-owned and -operated) enterprises could and did enter into market-exchange relationships with private capitalist corporations located, say, in Europe. China's socialist enterprises (i.e., state-owned and -operated) today engage in market exchanges with private capitalist enterprises inside and outside China. There are many such examples, because many existing national economies include more than one kind of economic system, and these different systems interact both nationally and internationally.

Socialist economic systems differ in important ways from capitalist systems, but here we must acknowledge that socialists disagree about those differences. Indeed, so do non-socialists, and often in similar ways. Since we will encounter these disagreements repeatedly in this book, we spell them out here.

One concept of socialism differentiates it from capitalism by the economic interventions of the state. For this concept of socialism, capitalism is a system of employers and employees such that both kinds of people have no position within the state. Thus their enterprises are referred to as "private." A capitalist economy exists if and when all or most enterprises producing and distributing resources and products are such private capitalist enterprises. Usually, in this view, the interactions among private enterprises, their hired laborers, and their customers are all exchanges in what this view labels a "free market." Like the word "private" applied to the enterprise, the word "free" applied to the market is meant to signal that the state as a social institution does not intervene (or intervenes minimally) in the production and distribution of goods and services.

Capitalism in this approach is defined as private enterprises plus free markets. It then follows that if and when a state intervenes or interferes in such private enterprises and/or free markets, capitalism is at least compromised or at most transformed into socialism. Since society intervenes through the agency of the state, this first kind of socialism names that "social intervention." Many libertarians, for example, believe that capitalism is compromised to the extent that it allows or admits state economic interventions. Where capitalism displays problems, libertarians' solutions tend to favor moving closer to the goals of fully private enterprises and free markets.

In this model, the extent of the state's intervention — from taxation and regulation to state-owned and -operated enterprises — defines the degree of socialism and its distance from capitalism. True, or "pure," capitalism exists when state interventions are near zero. For some variants of this perspective, socialism exists when the state's interventions are substantial or pervasive. For other variants, socialism exists in each individual state economic intervention: a government-run post office, a minimum wage imposed on employers, a progressive individual income tax, and so on. This latter perspective leads to notions that modern capitalism is actually a "mixed" system in which capitalism and socialism co-exist.

There are disagreements among proponents of these different variants. An example of great importance over the last century concerns the following debate: If the state merely regulates enterprises that otherwise remain private (owned and operated by private citizens with no position in the state apparatus), this is *not* socialism. Only if the state additionally owns and operates enterprises, at least within major sectors of the economy (sometimes called "the commanding heights"), does socialism exist. For decades, many referred to the Soviet Union as "socialist" because most of its industries were dominated by state-owned and -operated enterprises. In contrast, people hesitated to apply "socialist" to countries where state economic interventions were considerable but mostly excluded state-owned and -operated enterprises. A variation on this sort of thinking called the latter "socialist" and the former "communist." This reflected the post-1917 split in world socialism over the USSR's embrace of state-owned and -operated industrial enterprises. Socialists critical of or opposed to the USSR's form of socialism kept the name "socialist" while those who saw the USSR as *the* model for post-capitalist socialism took the name "communist." That split proved very influential in much thinking about capitalism versus socialism across the 20th century.

"Communism" became the widely accepted name for that kind of socialism that went beyond taxation and regulation to add the all-important direct state ownership and operation of enterprises. The socialists who joined and built communist parties advocated going beyond taxation, government spending on public services, and regulation to include state ownership and operation of many or all enterprises. Other socialists instead celebrated private, market capitalism where the state taxed, spent, regulated, and redistributed income and wealth more equally but did not own and operate many enterprises. The parties of such folk kept the "socialist" name and often stressed their commitments to political freedoms and civil liberties — in contrast to the practices of the communist systems, first in the USSR and later elsewhere as well.

The Great Depression of 1929–1941 added more layers of controversy and confusion around the name "socialism." The depth and duration of that capitalist crash provoked a whole new economics named after John Maynard Keynes. This new economics was devoted to rescuing capitalism from itself by both explaining the causes of capitalism's depressions and also offering policies (monetary and fiscal) to moderate, contain, and limit them. These were policies designed to be implemented by state authorities like central banks or government treasurers intervening in the economy.

Champions of capitalism were often horrified by Keynesian economics. To many, such policies seemed yet another assault on private enterprise and free markets, another celebration of state intervention in the economy, another kind of socialism. These people scoffed at Keynesians' frequent response that they aimed to save capitalism from itself. Keynesians insisted that the recurring depressions afflicting private capitalism, if not moderated by Keynesian state interventions, would eventually turn the working class against capitalism and thus end it. Keynes's pro-capitalist critics feared the power of the state more than the risk of recurring depressions. Despite Keynes's own repeated rejection of and distaste for socialism, communism, Marxism, and so on, to this day many closely associate Keynesian economics with socialism.

The issue of the state has always loomed large in defining socialism and its difference from capitalism. Modern capitalism came into the world oppressed and limited by the absolute monarchies of late European feudalism. Eventually, capitalism opposed these monarchies and then overthrew them. In France, the antagonist of the 1789 revolution was King Louis XVI; the American Revolution targeted King George III. Late feudalism's strong states were feared enemies. But anxieties about strong states persisted in capitalism long after feudalism had been defeated and discarded.

The reason for these anxieties was and remains mass or universal suffrage. When working-class people become the majority of voters electing parliaments and other state officials, capitalism's champions sense trouble and risk. Employees may and likely will blame their suffering (unemployment, low wages, bad working conditions, poor housing, etc.) on capitalist employers. Employees will recognize that their votes can empower a state apparatus to reduce or end that suffering. Tax structures, regulations of enterprises and markets, and other state interventions in the capitalist system can alter the distributions of income, wealth, and power from what they would be without such state interventions. Universal suffrage can enable the majority (employees) to offset the inequalities flowing from a capitalist economy dominated by a minority (employers). For the champions of private capitalism, the risks of a state powerful enough to impose taxes, regulations, and wealth redistribution through universal suffrage is as frightening now as feudal absolute monarchies were at capitalism's birth.

Modern capitalism wrestles with a contradiction: It needs a strong state apparatus — for coordination, external and internal security, managing externalities and the business cycle, and so on — and it fears the same. In the wake of the Great Depression in the US, public opinion favored state interventions such as the New Deal. Forty years later, the so-called Reagan revolution ushered in a neoliberalism that sought to minimize state interventions in the economy. After the 2008 crash of capitalism, economists Paul Krugman and Joseph Stiglitz are urging a re-evaluation of the benefits of state intervention.

But not everyone agrees. Capitalism's history did not produce only one socialist opposition with a shared focus on the state;

36

it also produced socialist dissenters. These dissenters also disliked capitalism and thought human society could and should do better, but they rejected the state and state intervention as the focal point of the contest between capitalism and socialism. While such dissenters have always hovered around the edges of the socialist movement, what brought them into the center of debate were the difficulties encountered by the early experiments in actual socialist economies. With an eye to the USSR after 1917, as early revolutionary enthusiasm and social transformations gave way first to Stalinism in the 1930s and then the implosion of 1989, the problematic relation of socialism to a powerful state took center stage. Many socialist critics of capitalism saw the state in the USSR as having itself become an obstacle to the kinds of social progress socialists championed. The social costs of the rapid economic development the USSR achieved were too large to deny or keep tolerating.

Views arose that the socialism of the USSR and its socialist allies had given the state too much power and transformed the rest of socialist society too little. The key questions became: Why did this failure happen, and what is to be done about it?

Struggling to answer these questions brought another kind of socialism to the forefront among socialists. In this interpretation of socialism, what defined it was less the role of the state in the economy, and more the *organization of production in the workplace.* The key issue of this kind of socialism is how human beings collaborate inside workplaces (factories, offices, stores) to produce the goods and perform the services that society needs or wants.

In capitalism, the participants in production are divided into employers and employees. In this alternative view of socialism, such should not be the case. The key term here is "should," because such a socialist organization of production has not yet been undertaken on a society-wide basis. Traditional socialisms concentrated on state activities — taxation, regulation, and state ownership and operation of workplaces — not on transforming the human relations within those workplaces. Indeed, traditional socialisms had taken over the basic employer-versus-employee organization of production from capitalism and changed it little if at all. Instead, socialist states taxed and regulated workplaces that had retained their capitalist organization (employer/employee) and sometimes also replaced private individuals with state officials as employers.

Socialist workplaces could and should be fundamentally different from capitalist workplaces in this alternative view of socialism. In capitalist workplaces, a small group (owners, boards of directors selected by owners, etc.) makes all the key decisions. In so doing, they are not accountable to the mass of employees or others affected by those decisions. In their internal organization, capitalist workplaces were and are still fundamentally undemocratic. They exclude majorities from power as surely and completely as monarchies exclude their subjects. The socialist alternative to capitalist organization entails the democratization of a workplace's internal structure. Every employee now has one constituent voice — equal to all other employees — in deciding what the workplace produces, what technology it uses, where production occurs, and what is done with the net revenues or surplus generated. In effect, in this model the employees become collectively their own employer. The age-old dichotomies of masters and slaves, lords and serfs, and employers and employees are finally displaced and overcome here. This conception of socialism thus represents a fundamental historical break from the slave, feudal, and capitalist systems.

In this perspective, socialism has pivoted from a largely macroeconomic to a primarily microeconomic focus. Socialism accomplishes the transition from capitalism by rebuilding the economy from the bottom up. Traditional socialisms never took this step on a society-wide basis of laying the foundation for an enduring economic system meant to replace capitalism. The early efforts at transition from capitalism to socialism stopped short at macro-changes — socializing means of production so they became state-owned and -operated, substituting centralized planning for markets as the major distributional mechanism, etc. — and never got to the micro-level. Traditional socialisms thus failed to target or include the micro-level democratic transformation of the workplace. That failure to complete the socialist revolution likely contributed to undermining the survival of those early, incomplete transitions from capitalism.

This is not surprising. Incomplete transitions have been the norm in the passages from slavery to feudalism or capitalism, from feudalism to capitalism, and so on. The emancipation of slaves during the US Civil War, for example, led to various subsequent relations of production — sharecropping, dependent tenancies, and so on — that fell far short of the economic freedom ex-slaves sought. Such was similarly the case with the early breaks from feudalism that led to capitalism.

Each economic system produces multiple forms that experience more or less successful transitions to new systems in different ways and at different paces. Many early experiments in transitioning from one economic system to another teach lessons that may help, if conditions permit, in assembling the means for a complete transition to a different system at some point in the future. There is little reason to expect that the transition from capitalism to socialism will be different in this respect. As has been the case with other economic transitions in history, the move away from capitalism has involved, and will continue to involve, more or less successful efforts, trials and errors, and steps forward and backward, until lessons learned combine with evolved conditions to enable the complete transition to socialism.

Socialists have learned crucial lessons from the Russian, Chinese, Cuban, and other revolutions of the 20th century. The economic systems constructed and tried by those revolutionaries have taught yet more lessons. The accumulated theories and practices of the socialist tradition have today been filtered through the conditions of a changing global capitalism to propel the tradition in new directions. Thus, today's socialism is characterized by both old notions and strategies, and new ones focused on democratizing workplaces.

Chapter III

Capitalism and Socialism: Struggles and Transitions

Human beings have had many different economic systems in their history. Transitions among them occurred in all directions. Changes in nature (climate, resource exhaustion, earthquakes, and so on) influenced those transitions, as did changes in technologies and social conflicts (wars, class struggles, migrations). Along the way in each particular system, beliefs that it was the final or permanent system eventually proved wrong.

Change is as continually present in economic systems as in everything else. Kinship or tribal economic systems, with collectively owned property alongside collective production and distribution of goods and services, gave way to private, individually owned and operated systems, and vice versa. Both of those sometimes gave way to slave systems, and again vice versa. Those in turn experienced transition to feudal (lord/serf) or capitalist (employer/employee) systems, and so on. Capitalist systems appeared and disappeared locally and repeatedly in human history before becoming regionally, nationally, and now globally prevalent. To imagine that today's capitalist system will last forever contradicts the history of every other system as well as of capitalist systems that arose and fell in the past. Hopefully, our collective knowledge of the different systems and transitions among them can limit and shape future transitions (as we seem to have done in precluding transitions back to slave and feudal systems).

No sooner did modern capitalism emerge in transitions out of feudalism and individual (self-employment) economic systems in Europe, out of a slave system in a large part of the US, and out of a variety of systems in the rest of the world, than it was challenged by another transition: socialism. Advocates of socialism sought transition beyond capitalism while capitalism's defenders tried to prevent any such change. Over the last two centuries a widespread theme of politics, economics, and culture was a struggle between advocates of capitalism and socialism over transitions between the systems. For most of the 19th century, capitalism seemed in the ascendancy; the possibility of transition to socialism, small. By the end of that century, that possibility had grown markedly stronger. Transition to socialism had become an explicit goal of socialist political parties then active in capitalism's major centers (Western Europe and North America). Across the 20th century, socialism shadowed capitalism around the world. Socialists in both colonizing (capitalist) and colonized (non-capitalist) territories began to see possibilities of transitions to socialism.

In nations where socialist or communist parties gained sufficient government power, transitions became official policy. Debates over the forms, mechanisms, and paces of transition proliferated. Debaters often took clues from what was known about earlier transitions between economic systems. Of particular interest was the transition from feudalism to capitalism in Europe after the 15th century.

The basic lessons drawn by socialists from past transitions between economic systems was captured in Marx's succinct phrase: "The history of all hitherto existing societies is the history of class struggles." Slavery was beset by struggles between masters and slaves, feudalism by struggles between lords and serfs, and capitalism by struggles between employers and employees. Those class struggles shaped the quality and history of each type of economic system and thus of the societies in which those systems existed. Class struggles are always key contributors to eventual transitions to different economic systems.

The feudal system had its internal contradictions that generated conflicts between lords and serfs over labor and rental obligations, soil exhaustion from feudal cultivation techniques, wars among lords, and so on. The struggles provoked by such contradictions produced two noteworthy results internal to European feudalism. The first was a transition in which a decentralized structure of lords and serfs on small and medium-sized manors gave way to increasingly large, concentrated manors organized as a hierarchy with a huge feudal manor at the top. The lords of those top manors became the kings of the so-called absolute monarchies of late European feudalism.

The second result of European feudalism's contradictions disconnected serfs from manors (via revolts, escapes, changed farming practices, etc.). Such displaced serfs lost their access to manorial resources, and thus urgently sought means of survival by finding and settling with other feudal outsiders. Among these were bands of outlaws living off plunder: the Robin Hood model. Other serfs, instead, joined with merchants: a group, neither lord nor serf, that existed by engaging in trade. Merchants exchanged goods with lords and serfs, often moving them from where they were relatively plentiful and cheap to where they were scarce and expensive. When merchants needed help to secure or expand their trading, they began to enter into a new and different relationship with serfs disconnected from feudal manors. They struck a deal: merchants advanced to disconnected serfs the means for their survival in exchange for the serfs providing their ability to work for the merchant as the merchant directed. Employer and employee came into existence alongside lord and serf.

In that deal, capitalism, a non-feudal economic system, arrived. It featured a new relationship in the production and distribution of goods and services different from the feudal one. In the feudal system, the serf was bound to the lord across generations. The bond — an intense personal connection of the serf and his/her family to the land and its feudal lord and lord's family — was all the stronger because church rituals sanctified it. In contrast, the employer and employee were both "free" persons bound by neither personal nor religious connection. Instead, they entered voluntarily into a contractual relation governing the exchange between them. They exchanged what was private property to each:

commodities or money owned by the employer (accumulated by the merchant) and the ability to do labor (or labor power) owned by the employee.

The employer purchased labor power and combined it (in production) with other inputs (tools, equipment, raw materials, etc.) likewise purchased by the employer. During production, the worker's labor added value to the value already embodied in the other inputs that got used up in production. The outputs of production contained a total value equal to the sum of the used-up inputs' value and the value added by the laborers. The employer sold the outputs and thereby obtained their value in exchange. Money was usually the measure and means of exchange.

With that total value in hand, the employer typically replaced the used-up inputs and paid the employee what had been contractually agreed upon: the wage. This typically left the employer with some "extra" or "surplus" value. That was because the value added by the worker usually exceeded the value of the wage paid to the worker. That excess was the employer's gain — often called "profit." Profit was the employers' incentive, their "bottom line," and thus capitalism's driving force. The concept of "capital" had long defined the use of money to make more money (as moneylenders and merchants did). Because the employer/employee production system did exactly that too, it came to be called "capitalism."

In this capitalist, employer/employee relationship in production, what the capitalist offered was privately owned wealth (perhaps inherited, stolen, accumulated from merchantry or moneylending, or saved from wages). But the capitalist only offered that wealth on condition that combining it with labor power in production would yield a surplus value for the capitalist. In other words, the seller of labor power needed to accept — knowingly or unknowingly — a payment (wage or salary) that had less value than what the worker's labor added to the other inputs used during the production process.

It is this core mechanism that generates struggles between employers and employees. Employers want to pay less value to workers to acquire their labor power. That is because the less paid to workers, the greater the surplus or excess of value added by the worker in production over the value paid for the worker's labor power. That surplus is the employer's goal and means of competitive survival. In contrast, workers want more value paid to them for their labor power, as that enables their standard of living and that of all others dependent upon them. Class struggles between employers and employees follow. They have dogged capitalism everywhere and throughout its history.

Sooner or later, European struggles between lords and serfs grew and matured from disputing only their respective obligations within the feudal system to questioning, challenging, and eventually overthrowing the feudal system itself. Along the way, revolutionary serfs found allies among the employers and employees that established enclaves of capitalism within the larger feudal society. Serfs seeking to leave feudal manors found refuge in the villages, towns, and cities where capitalist economic relationships existed and were accepted. The latter grew accordingly and so did the threat they represented to feudal lords, who often crushed the many large and small capitalist experiments in those villages and towns (e.g., Emperor Frederick I's wars against the city-states of northern Italy in the 12th century). There were centuries of trials and errors, countless efforts to construct and sustain capitalist economic systems surrounded by more or less hostile feudal manors (e.g., the enclosures in Britain). Slowly a reluctant feudalism accepted co-existence with a rising capitalism. Eventually, the capitalist employers and employees allied with increasingly anti-feudal serfs to make revolutions against absolute feudal monarchs and thereby complete the transition from feudalism to capitalism.

A parallel pattern characterizes the growth and maturation of capitalism's struggles between employees and employers. Socialism is the form that maturity took. Socialism represents the awareness of employees that their sufferings and limitations come less from the employers than from the capitalist system. It is that system that prescribes for both sides the incentives and options, the rewards and punishments for their behavioral "choices." It is that system that generates their endless struggles and the employees' slow-dawning realization that system change — transition from capitalism to socialism — is the way out.

Most employers have understood for a long time that socialists were their enemies. Even as socialists' ideas changed, what they wanted for employees seemed almost always to be contrary to what employers wanted or felt they could tolerate. In the 19th and 20th centuries, when socialists seemed to want more state economic intervention, employers mostly feared where that might lead in terms of constricting their freedom to profit from employing workers. Only during capitalist depressions (especially the 1930s) or when socialist political movements were very strong did employers relent and make some concessions to keep the capitalist system in place. Faced with the rapid rise of socialism in Germany, Otto von Bismarck and his successors undertook a state welfare system and eventually allowed labor unions. In the US, socialism's rise likewise propelled Franklin Roosevelt to legalize labor unions; begin Social Security, unemployment insurance, and massive federal jobs programs; as well as institute a minimum wage.

In both these cases, however, the basic capitalist employer-versus-employee system was maintained. Socialist movements, organizations, political parties, and spokespersons were repeatedly silenced, imprisoned, and crushed. International opposition and isolation greeted the Soviet Union after 1917 and the People's Republic of China after 1949. The US after World War II and Germany after 1968 purged many socialists from government, academic, and other social institutions. The US under Trump has been trying to revive an anti-Chinese bloc since 2018. For at least the last century, socialist efforts to mount political movements, take power, and develop socialist economic systems have suffered ideological, political, economic, and military destruction around the world. This was usually led by the US in an effort to protect capitalism and the democracy and freedom it allegedly generates.

Over more or less the same time period, the transition from capitalism to socialism was seen, from both sides, as a movement from a system of private enterprises and markets to a system of state enterprises and state planning. With some important exceptions, that movement seemed ascendant from 1917 to 1989, while the reverse movement has seemed dominant since. The implosion of the USSR seemed the nodal turning point.

Most socialists celebrated the transition from private to state enterprises and from markets to planning as central components of building a new socialist society. They were optimistic that society's ownership of the means of production by the state and planned distribution of resources and products by the state would finally end the unequal distributions of income and wealth typical of capitalism. It would similarly avoid capitalist instability by preventing business cycles through government planning. The irrationality of unemployment would be eliminated, and technological advances would enable a growing shift from work to leisure within each day. Freedom would then come to mean freedom from exploitation because work itself was reduced as a portion of one's life and because the workers were producing surpluses not for others (i.e., the employer/capitalist class), but rather for their own representatives in a democratic workers' state.

In contrast, advocates for capitalism saw transitions to socialism as retreats from the freedoms and standards of living achieved by capitalism. Workers in socialism, they warned, would have only one employer and thus lack the freedom to leave one employer for another, which existed in private capitalism. More problematic still, they argued, was the power concentrated in the proposed socialism's state apparatus (especially when one, single political party controlled that apparatus). It would be the owner and operator of workplaces, the planner who distributed resources among them, and the distributor of outputs among all who wanted them. Such concentrated economic power within the state could make it dictatorial within socialist societies, thus extinguishing civil liberties and individual rights. Critics of socialism along these lines characterized the state powers inside the USSR, the People's Republic of China, Vietnam, Cuba, and so on, as dictatorships.

The 20th century's "great debate" between capitalism and socialism was distinguished by the former's private enterprises and markets versus the latter's public enterprises and central planning. Where governments taxed and regulated private capitalist enterprises (but did not own and operate them) and regulated markets (but did not replace them with planning), the term "socialist" was retained. In contrast, "communist" designated that kind of socialism in which state-owned and - operated enterprises prevailed and markets either disappeared or were controlled by central planning authorities. "Socialist" thus came to be used for many countries in Scandinavia, other parts of Western Europe, and Asia. "Communist" described countries like the USSR and its Eastern European allies, the People's Republic of China, Vietnam, Cuba, and so on. These usages were not universally agreed upon, but they were more widespread than alternative usages.

On one level that great debate ended in 1989 with the implosion of the USSR and its Eastern European allies, along with major economic changes in many of the other communist economies. A kind of capitalist triumphalism advanced the idea that capitalism had won and socialism had lost. For many of capitalism's enthusiasts "no alternative" could outcompete capitalism. A kind of "end of history" had set in so far as economic systems were concerned. However, the great crash of 2008 (capitalism's second worst after the Great Depression of the 1930s) showed that capitalist triumphalism was mistaken. Criticisms of capitalism resumed alongside heightened class struggles.

Also after 1989, many socialists felt the need to explain what had caused the implosion of the 20th century's efforts to construct socialist economies in Eastern Europe. Explanations emerged and sometimes extended to asking whether the very notions of socialism needed to be re-examined. Might there need to be changes in 21st-century socialism's goals and strategies based on lessons learned from its 20th-century experiments and efforts? A debate arose among socialists that continues to the present. Broadly speaking, one side holds on to the 20th-century conventions: that socialism entails either the socialization of the means of production plus central planning, or a democratic government that regulates private capitalism and markets for social goals. The other side criticizes both those conventions, claiming they may not be necessary and they are definitely not sufficient. With or without socialized ownership and planning or government regulation, 21st-century socialism focuses on and prioritizes something else — namely, the transformation of workplaces from capitalism's hierarchical internal structures to fully democratic worker cooperatives.

The focus of the capitalism-versus-socialism debate is being basically challenged by the changes within socialism. The role of the state is no longer the central issue in dispute. Who the employers are (private citizens or state officials) now matters far less than what kind of relationship exists between employers and employees in the workplace. Are they different groups of people such that one hires/fires the other, one produces a surplus and the other appropriates it, one makes all the key decisions and the other either accepts them without participating in them or else leaves to find employment in another, similarly organized workplace? Or are they cooperative workplaces where the collective of all workers democratically makes the key decisions: what, how, and where to produce; how to use profits; and what wages/salaries to pay each individual worker/collective member?

Socialism is shifting such that one of its priority goals is the transition of workplaces from capitalist hierarchies to democratic cooperatives. This prioritized goal is to be added to and emphasized alongside the conventional socialist priority goals. That is, socialism is becoming the movement to build a new society with equally important new macroeconomic and microeconomic institutions. In such a society, new macroeconomic institutions will have likely transitioned from private to a mix of state and regulated private ownership, and likely from relatively "free" market distribution to a mix of planning (centralized or decentralized) and regulated market exchanges. Its new microeconomic institutions will have transitioned from capitalist, hierarchical ones to democratic worker co-ops. Socialism will mean and require the advocacy of social change toward, and the building of, a society in which both these macro and micro transitions are underway and have been significantly achieved.

At a certain stage in their development, feudal class struggles between lords and serfs became about more than the specifics of their relationship (sizes of feudal dues, rents, corvée labor obligations, and so on). They began to focus on the feudal class relationship as a whole and began to conceptualize alternative relations of production and correspondingly different societies built on them. As struggling serfs grew in consciousness and self-confidence, they also gained a certain space and acceptance for the alternative capitalist system to co-exist inside feudalism. Eventually transition occurred, often punctuated by revolutions such as the ones that occurred in England, America, and France in the 17th and 18th centuries.

In the 21st-century socialism discussed above, a similar transitional trajectory is envisioned. Within capitalism, employer/employee struggles are resuming after their declines in the second half of the 20th century. Quickly they are maturing from capitalism's specifics to systemic concerns with socialist alternatives. Interest in, and formations of, worker co-ops are growing fast, as is the self-confidence of socialists.

This is remarkable for two major reasons. First, the two great experiments in transitions beyond private capitalism in the 20th century – Russia and China – have yielded a rich crop of lessons, precedents to build on, and tragic detours to avoid. Resuming the effort of a transition to socialism entails close attention to those lessons. Second, those two experiments contributed to two great reactionary purges that targeted socialism in the 20th century: fascism before World War II and anti-communism afterwards. The legacies of those purges continue to impact socialism today, creating both obstacles and opportunities for the transition to socialism in the years ahead. In any case, that transition is once again front and center on the historical agenda.

Chapter IV

Russia and China: Major Experiments in Constructing Socialism

Socialism took a huge step when socialists achieved, for the first time, what so many socialists had long wished for. In 1917 socialists in Russia emerged from the chaos of the czar's loss in World War I with an effective combination of revolutionary theory, strategies, and tactics. A small, well-organized political party enabled them to "seize the state." From that position they undertook to construct what they understood to be the world's first socialist government and society, the Union of Soviet Socialist Republics (USSR).

From a set of utopian dreams of a world better than that provided by early capitalism, socialism had grown with (and because of) capitalism to become its systemic critic. Along the way, socialist criticism developed both theoretical and practical expressions: the British Chartists, Proudhon's ideas,

Marx's life's work, the Revolutions of 1848, the German Socialist Party. A groundswell of people, their organizations and activities, built 19th-century socialism into a formidable international movement of social criticism and opposition to capitalism.

Then, in the 1917 Russian Revolution and its aftermath, socialism added something new and different. "Socialism" began not only to mean the most developed, systematic critique of capitalism, but also to refer to constructing, operating, and governing a post-capitalist economic system and society. Something barely begun and lasting only weeks in the Paris Commune of 1871 was rethought and refashioned in Russia in 1917. It lasted for over 70 years.

In undertaking the experiment of building a socialist alternative to capitalism, socialism changed itself profoundly. For example, with the beginning of the experiment, socialism split into communism and socialism over profound disagreements. Ever since 1917, socialists and communists offered different but overlapping critiques of capitalism. They differed also in their evaluations of the new socialist economies constructed first in, and later also beyond, the USSR.

From the beginning, the new USSR's survival and growth provoked opposition and anxiety in socialism's enemies, both inside Russia and internationally. The pro-monarchist, ultra-nationalistic "White Russians" allied with foreign governments, resulting in a civil war and an invasion by foreign troops (British, French, Japanese, and American) aimed at defeating the experiment. Innovation and hostility shaped much of the USSR's first decades.

Later in the century, in 1949, socialists in China undertook a similar experiment. Revolution took them from an oppositional force targeting Chinese capitalism to a revolutionary government determined to construct a new, post-capitalist economic system: the People's Republic of China (PRC). In some ways, China's socialists replicated inside the PRC the Soviet experiment inside the USSR. For example, as in the USSR, Chinese socialism operated mostly within a communist party and focused on state ownership of the means of industrial production and state central planning. In other ways, however, China's development as a socialist economy and society took different directions. For example, since the 1980s, China has increasingly enabled large private capitalist enterprises, foreign and domestic, to operate inside the PRC, and relied on exports and the world market.

Together, the USSR and the PRC have represented the most important national experiments in constructing a socialist economic system and society. As the largest countries by geography (USSR) and by population (PRC), they exemplified how far socialism had come in the historically short span of under two centuries. Together, they showed how capitalism's global expansion beyond Europe had been matched by socialism's. The results of these two experiments had, and continue to have, immense impacts on socialism and capitalism today.

In this book, our approach to the USSR and China focuses on their relationships to an evolving socialism. We seek to avoid

Cold War denunciations and apologies that so often badly distorted debates over these topics as each side demonized the other and celebrated itself. Much of the literature since 1945, and even after the implosions of Eastern European socialisms in 1989, repeats those lopsided themes. Of course, every writer's partisanship influences what gets written. Our perspective should by now be clear. We aim to offer a non-dogmatic, nuanced assessment of the two greatest experiments to date in constructing socialist economies.

The Union of Soviet Socialist Republics (USSR)

In the century before 1917, Russia was a mostly feudal society in a painful transition to capitalism. In that process, feudalism was only officially abolished in 1863, and the capitalism that emerged included a large component of foreign-owned firms. When Russia entered World War 1 in 1914, it was still a transitional economy with significant feudal remnants; a fast-growing capitalist sector; and many tensions among landlords, capitalists, ex-serf peasants, and an urban working class. The extreme inequalities among them and widespread desperate poverty had already exploded earlier in 1904-5, when both a war with Japan was lost and a revolution convulsed large areas of Russia. Thus, Russia's defeat in World War I finally undermined the autocratic czarist government at a moment when an emerging capitalism was still relatively new, brutal, small, and vulnerable to competing capitalists in far stronger European countries.

Desperate wartime conditions, extreme inequality, and poverty, coupled with czarist censorship and repression battling winds of parliamentary democracy and socialism from the West, combined to produce a revolutionary explosion in 1917. The czarist regime collapsed, and the Russian capitalists were too weak politically to form a durable replacement government. The socialist-party faction (Bolsheviks) that led the revolution had learned lessons from the 1905 revolt (chiefly, the need to build an alliance with a revolutionary party among the peasant majority). It had also established a significant presence in the small industrial Russian working class. Its anti-capitalist message gathered the political strength necessary to wage the 1917 revolution and establish the USSR as a new society with a new socialist government.

For some, the survival and growth of the new Soviet society was a kind of validation of socialist movements everywhere. It was seen that socialists could overturn a hostile government. Socialists could capture state power and make it serve in the transition from capitalism to socialism. Others went further: They saw the USSR as the embryo of a global socialist future. It was an embryo to be nurtured and supported as a priority for socialists everywhere. Still others worried that the Soviet version of socialism could or already did clash with the values and commitments of other socialists. The victorious Bolshevik faction had long struggled with opposing factions inside Russian socialism. The milestone represented by the Soviet revolution sharpened differences that had been maturing inside 19th-century socialism.

Among these differences were deep divisions over how to utilize state power, once captured, to bring about the transition to socialism. One side advocated peaceful, parliamentary politics, while the other advocated revolutionary breakthroughs. Other differences concerned civil liberties and tolerance for dissent in societies governed by socialists, democratic governance of workplaces and residential communities, and commitments to internationalism. Key aspects of the new USSR became flashpoints for disagreement. Was the concept of a "dictatorship of the proletariat" a shorthand to define a government's class priorities or a description of how socialist governors treated the governed? Was socialism necessarily a transnational movement and society, or could there be "socialism in one country"? Were anarchists allies or enemies of socialism?

These and still other disagreements among socialists around the world reacting to the USSR produced the profound split mentioned earlier. Those who stayed with the idea that the USSR represented socialism's future and deserved basic support by socialists everywhere broke away from global socialism and took the name "communist." Those who were more or less critical of the kind of socialism being constructed in the USSR kept the name "socialist." In the early 1920s many existing socialist political parties split along these lines. The socialist movement thereafter included both socialist and communist political parties. The split provoked parallel divisions among self-identified socialists outside political parties as well.

In the first decade after the 1917 revolution, the USSR had to face the fact that, as the only country with a government committed to socialism, it was alone in the world. Efforts at parallel revolutionary breaks elsewhere in Europe (Hungary, Bavaria, etc.) had not succeeded. Extraordinary efforts and sacrifices enabled the Bolsheviks to win the civil war and their newly formed Communist Party of the Soviet Union to retain leadership.

The early Soviet leadership under Lenin had to grapple with multiple, threatening crises from the outset: near-total isolation within a hostile world of capitalism, extreme poverty, urgent needs to recover from the war, and complicated splits between communists and socialists within and outside the USSR.

Lenin himself admitted that socialism was a goal, not yet an achieved reality. A socialist party had taken political power, but it still had not used that power to transform capitalism into a very different socialism. As Lenin put it, they had achieved "state capitalism." That is, a socialist party had state power, and the state had become the industrial capitalist displacing the former private capitalists. But Soviet society was still capitalist in the employer-employee organization of its economy. He hoped and worked to guide that state capitalism into a transition to socialism.

But when Lenin died in 1924, the new leadership that emerged (and remained into the 1950s) revolved around Stalin. The Stalinist period was a period of nearly constant crises. Foreign hostilities were problems from the beginning. The 1929 capitalism crash provoked a rising right-wing political movement (e.g., Nazism and other fascisms) that targeted Bolshevism. Internally, the initial revolutionary distribution of land to the peasants had produced a peasantry — the majority inside the USSR — with quite different goals and objectives than those of the government. Stalin's state saw rapid industrialization as the top Soviet priority, in order to: (1) defend the USSR's socialism against the hostile industrialized economies threatening it from outside; (2) deliver on the political promise to rapidly modernize Soviet society as a whole; and (3) recover from the damages of World War I, revolution, civil war, and foreign invasions (1914 to 1922).

Stalinism came to be the name for the Soviet government's harsh, sometimes violent, determination to achieve these goals against any and all opposition, real and often imagined. This entailed constricting consumption to free the maximum possible resources for industrialization. Stalinism also constricted civil liberties; artistic expression; theoretical debates over socialism's diverse interpretations; and many early Soviet experiments in politics, culture, and economics where revolutionaries sought to institutionalize concepts of socialism. For example, initial Soviet experiments to free women from the subordination and drudgeries of patriarchal households inherited from the feudal and capitalist past were abandoned as "socially too disruptive," in much the same way as the Soviets renounced the early efforts at democratizing workplaces. Amid Stalinism's pressures, questioning basic Soviet strategy became taboo. The benefits of Stalinism in preparing for and defeating Hitler's attack, in rapid industrialization, etc., have been debated against Stalinism's internal costs in political repression, cultural uniformity, neglect of agriculture, etc., to this day.

The development of the USSR, led by its Communist Party, has sharpened certain differences among socialists — often expressed by disagreements between socialists and communists — since the 1920s. Many socialists outside the USSR pursued a transition beyond capitalism by means of parliamentary politics. Their socialist parties embraced peaceful change, to be achieved by winning elections. Once the state apparatus had been won for the socialist party, it would proceed to shift ownership of the means of production from private to state. However, this would be a long, slow process during which private capitalist enterprises would co-exist with a slowly expanding state sector. At the same time, the socialist state would regulate or replace market exchange with its own centrally planned distribution of resources and products. That, too, would be a long, slow process.

Other socialists formed other socialist parties that promoted a shorter, faster transitional path. They formulated programs of rapid nationalization of industry, deeper market regulation, and more systemic planning. They foresaw the need for a rapid redistribution of wealth and income to solidify their political base as well as a speedy transition. They generally wanted more extensive and rapid implementation of the following: rising minimum wages; progressive taxation of property and income; and subsidized national health care, housing, education, and transport.

In contrast, communists and the communist parties they organized advocated a socialism that insisted on more or less immediate state ownership and operation of most, or at least "the commanding heights," of industry, and often parts of agriculture too. The USSR, for example, despite keeping the word "socialist" in the country's name, followed the communist model and nationalized most industries and, after 1930, an important part of agriculture ("state farms"). After World War II, the communist model based on the Soviet experience tended to be followed by many new socialist governments in Asia (China and Vietnam), Europe (the USSR's Eastern European allies), and Latin America (Cuba). Communist political parties around the world — loosely connected in "Communist Internationals" — celebrated the Soviet model and criticized the socialist alternative. The socialists generally did the reverse.

Despite the socialist/communist split, many on both sides endorsed the old, pre-split idea that socialism was the first stage of the transition beyond capitalism, whereas communism was a later stage. Some held socialism to be an in-between stage: no longer capitalist but not yet communist. A remark by Marx often served to summarize the difference: In socialism, the rule governing work and the distribution of income is "from each according to his/her ability and to each according to his/her work." In communism it will be "from each according to his/her ability and to each according to his/her need." Such shared perspectives help explain why Soviet-type economies often run by communist parties called their economies "socialist" (as both the USSR and PRC consistently did). Likewise, where socialists governed economies that retained a mostly private capitalist system (for example, many countries in Western Europe at various times) in a slow and uneven transition, their socialist parties also referred to their own economies as "socialist."

The actual economic history of the USSR has been far more complex than one might guess from the Cold War depictions dominating the literature. For example — and contrary to the idea that communists always reject private property — one of the first acts of the new Soviet government formed in 1917 was to divide and give land to the mass of landless peasants *as their private property.* At that point, land was by far the most important "means of production" in the economy. Even after the later collectivization of agriculture around 1930 (when state farms began their steady growth in importance), the many "collective farms" were private, not state, operations. In addition, Stalin had to allow effective private property on the peasants' "individual plots." The notion that the USSR banned all private property is false.

Likewise, the notion that the USSR eliminated markets in favor of central planning is false. What did happen was that widespread market transactions were allowed and encouraged within the larger framework of a central economic plan. Some market exchanges occurred at prices set administratively by planners, while others were freely negotiated among buyers and sellers. Across Soviet history, policies came and went that gave more or less freedom to market exchanges relative to central plans.

Rejecting Cold War caricatures still leaves the problem of deciding how best to characterize the actual economic system in the USSR. Was it genuinely post-capitalist, and if so, was it socialist? If it was not socialist, what was it? Given the central role played by the USSR in the 20th century's so-called great debate between capitalism and socialism, deciding what the

USSR actually was is to take a position in and on that debate as well.

In the wake of the 1917 revolution, the new Soviet government took actions drawn from the thinking and the platforms of 19th-century European socialism. It nationalized industry (but not agriculture). It closed the stock market. It established a central government economic-planning institution charged with organizing the distribution of resources among workplaces, and products among the workplaces and consumers who wanted them. It established regulations and goals that drove the economy to (1) recover from the devastations of 1914-1922, (2) build up industrial capacity to overcome economic underdevelopment and military vulnerabilities, and (3) provide rising standards of living for the population. In place of profit maximization for capitalists and elite consumption standards for Russia's top one percent, the Soviet system prioritized industrialization and growth. It proved far more successful at achieving goals (1) and (2) than (3).

But were industries in the USSR socialist or capitalist? If the criterion to answer this question is whether they were owned and operated by private citizens or state officials, then they were socialist, because the Soviet state owned and operated them. Suppose instead that the criterion is whether the relations of production were hierarchical and dichotomous in the private capitalist manner: an employer minority hired an employee majority. Then the Soviet industrial system would have to be deemed capitalist since a minority of persons — Soviet state officials — functioned as employers of an employee majority. It would be *state* capitalism because the employers were state officials and thus different from *private* capitalism where employers are NOT state officials.

There is no question that Soviet industry was predominantly hierarchical and dichotomous. In Soviet industrial workplaces, a state official was placed in the position of employer, through the agency of leaders of the state and the Communist Party. In private capitalism, the position of employer is occupied either by the individual(s) who own(s) and organize(s) the workplace or by corporate boards of directors elected by shareholders with one vote per share owned.

The Soviet revolution had changed who the employer was; it had not ended the employer/employee relationship. In place of private capitalism, the Soviet revolution had established a state capitalism.

The notion that capitalism displays both state and private forms should come as no surprise. Historically, the slave and feudal economic systems before modern capitalism likewise displayed both private and state forms. Alongside or instead of private masters who owned slaves, states and state officials could and did own slaves. Local feudal lords across medieval Europe had serfs, but so did the lords who operated as state officials, e.g., kings. Historians do not find the presence of state forms of slavery or feudalism alongside (or instead of) their private forms as signs that those societies no longer deserve the labels slave or feudal — quite the contrary. Capitalism, too, displays both private and state forms in varying proportions.

The USSR constructed a largely state-capitalist economy. Given its early circumstances — poverty and economic underdevelopment, war and post-war economic destruction, global isolation and hostility — state capitalism was as far as Lenin and others felt they could proceed toward socialism. Socialists had achieved a revolutionary government and taken control of a major nation's industry. They were in a good position to make the further transition from state capitalism to socialism.

During the 1920s, the USSR achieved economic recovery from the disasters of 1914-1922. It also allowed and supported private enterprises, especially merchants and farmers, under what Lenin named the New Economic Policy (NEP). By the end of the 1920s, those private enterprises had grown. Some remained self-employed individuals, while others became small capitalists (an employer/employee structure). Under Stalin, however, private interests and the Stalinist notion of a transition from capitalism to socialism clashed. The Soviet government then suppressed much of what Lenin's NEP had produced. It collectivized agriculture, pressing the peasants who had acquired their own land in the 1917 revolution into newly organized private collective farms and state farms. Many of those peasants — and especially those who had become richer and often employers of others who had lost their land — resisted collectivization as a program depriving them of their private property. Stalin's government responded harshly, and violence ensued as collectivization was completed. On collective farms, farmers sometimes functioned as small self-employed individuals and sometimes as small, medium, or even large cooperatives. The structures of these agricultural cooperatives sometimes came very close to having workers become the collective owners and operators of their farms. The collective farms often reproduced the employer/employee structure of capitalism

68

with the difference that employees had some (varying) influence on the employers. In contrast, Soviet state farms adopted the same employer/employee structure that had been established in industry: state capitalism. For many years, private collective and state farms co-existed in the USSR.

However, so strong was the attachment of Soviet farmers to "their own piece of land" that such pieces were set aside for them on collective and state farms. These were, in effect, the private property of individual farmers (and their families) who could work them, sell the produce in local markets, and retain the resulting revenues. Thus, the Soviet class structure was indeed complicated. State capitalism in industry and agriculture co-existed with private self-employment and collective/cooperative systems across large parts of the agricultural sector. In addition, an underground (legal and illegal) economy exhibited self-employed individuals, small capitalists, and small worker co-ops. Regulating this economy was a powerful state that included a central planning apparatus and also an intrusive Communist Party apparatus.

As an engine of rapid economic development with emphasis on industry, Soviet state capitalism was remarkably successful. The USSR's growth took it from being one of Europe's poorest regions devastated by war in 1917 to being the world's number-two superpower by the 1960s. Moreover, that achievement occurred despite massive destruction in the USSR from both World Wars, revolution, civil war, foreign invasions, and a violent agricultural collectivization. The prices paid for such growth included an underdeveloped agriculture; limited real-wage gains; many unmet consumer needs; and continued constraints on civil liberties, political freedoms, etc., under Stalin's nearly 30 years of dictatorial leadership.

The generation and reinvestment of huge surpluses enabled Soviet industrialization. Some of those surpluses were realized within the industrial sector. Some came from keeping wages low while continuously boosting worker productivity. And some came from unequal exchanges between industry and agriculture by means of planners keeping administered prices of agricultural staples (chiefly grains) low relative to the industrial products farmers bought (tractors, implements, fertilizers, etc.). These planning and industrial management decisions shaped the costs incurred for the industrial growth achieved.

Lenin's hope that a socialist government plus state capitalism would enable and suffice for a further transition from state capitalism to socialism proved premature. A decade after the revolution, it was clear that much more had to be done to lift Soviet industry to the point where an adequate economy could support an adequate military so both could survive surrounded by a hostile capitalist world. To that end, Soviet workers would need to continue to work for low real wages, and agriculture would continue to be squeezed — both to fund more industrialization. The difficult forced march of Soviet development, pressured by time, continued.

In that situation, Stalin and his advisers made a fateful decision that has shaped socialism's global history since. Breaking decisively with Lenin, Stalin declared socialism to have been achieved in the USSR. No further references to state capitalism in the USSR would be tolerated. Socialism was no longer the goal of a transitional period that would, in turn, give way to a transition to communism. Instead socialism was the here and now. Socialism was the USSR and vice versa. Communism was effectively banished to so distant a future as to be irrelevant here and now.

It thus became easier for socialism's critics and enemies to attack socialism. One could quote Stalin to equate socialism with the USSRs ongoing problems: constrained real wages, squeezed agriculture, absent civil liberties and political freedoms. Before, those lamentable conditions had characterized a transitional period before socialism was achieved. But after Stalin's decision to "declare" socialism achieved, those conditions became definitions of socialism. Critics made a habit of repeating the equation endlessly. The strategy of socialism's enemies became simple and obvious: First use military threats, economic sanctions, covert interventions, and political isolation to worsen the conditions of a nation run by socialists, and then identify those conditions with socialism.

After 1945, the Cold War, with its arms race and global confrontations, took a huge toll on the USSR. Before then it might have hoped to free up some of its surplus for investment to provide increased private consumption for workers through higher real wages and to fund better collective, subsidized consumption. The wartime alliance with the US, UK, and France against Nazi Germany likely encouraged such hopes. But after the alliance came the Cold War, and Soviet leaders instead invested still more in very expensive armaments (including nuclear), in costly military campaigns (Afghanistan), and foreign support projects (Cuba).

After 1945, Western, primarily US, mass media (especially television and cinema) spread and expanded their reach into the USSR. After the 1960s, their reach further increased and brought abundant evidence of levels of mass consumption much higher in the West than in the USSR, and higher also than what Soviet mass media had led Soviet citizens to expect about Western mass consumption. Food, clothing, apartments, cars, and furnishings shown widely available to working people in the West stimulated pent-up demand in the USSR. That plus later-reduced US-USSR tensions stimulated the repressed demands of Soviet workers and citizens for more consumer goods, civil liberties, and freedoms. But the pressures on the Soviet surplus to fund further industrialization, plus the direct and indirect costs of the Cold War at the same time, precluded meeting those demands. Soviet workers reacted by shifting their focus from state and collective workplaces to their private plots and under-the-table economic activities. That depressed workers' productivity in state and collective workplaces, depressing their incomes there and further shifting attention to private plots, etc. This vicious cycle provoked the Communist Party to try to suppress workers and deny their betrayal and disappointment. Opposition to the limits on consumption, civil liberties, and freedoms built toward an explosion that burst into the open in 1989.

In Marxist economic theory, one approach to explaining economic history compares the supply of surplus (what remains from output after wages are paid and used-up means of production are replaced) and a society's demands on that surplus. In other words, will the surplus suffice to increase workers' consumption, expand industrial and agricultural capacities (i.e., accumulate capital, fund research and development, etc.), serve the military's needs, allow for exports to pay for imports, and so on? If the society's demands for surplus distributions exceed their supply, difficult social decisions must be made. Whatever those decisions are, portions of the population will emerge unsatisfied. Depending on the conditions and context, unsatisfied people may turn in anger against the system.

Whether they do so depends in part on how they view the system in place and how it compares to alternative systems. Stalin's decision to describe the USSR as "socialism achieved" was never definitively renounced or rejected subsequently, even when Stalin's dictatorship was. So as the gap between supply and demands on surplus in Soviet state capitalism built toward explosion, popular dissatisfaction grew. Sometimes Soviet dissidents targeted individual leaders, such as Leonid Brezhnev, sometimes artistic censorship and insufficient civil liberties. As repression or uninterest by government worsened, popular anger shifted toward bureaucratic corruption, then Communist Party failures, and eventually the socialist system itself.

Because successive Soviet regimes had blocked the educational system, mass media, and political debates from admitting and discussing alternative concepts of socialism and socialist economic systems, most Soviet people believed there were but two alternative systems. Socialism was what they knew in the USSR. In contrast, capitalism had been the object of endless criticism. However, after the 1960s, with mass media, freer travel, and *détente* (i.e., reduced tensions between the US and USSR), people in the USSR came to understand that workers in many capitalist countries enjoyed far greater standards of living than the USSR, as well as greater civil liberties and freedoms.

Increasing numbers of Soviet people began to think critically about their system (which they knew as "socialism") and to favor a transition to the one "other" system that seemed possible: capitalism as in the US or Western Europe. As the system they had became unbearable, so they went toward the only other system they recognized.

We can see something similar happening in the United States, but in the opposite direction. Since 2008's economic crash, increasing numbers of young Americans have ever-more-limited economic options and unsustainable college debts; plus they find the political system completely out-of-touch, serving only the elites. Endless celebration of the status quo has taught them that the broken system is capitalism. So they, like their Soviet counterparts of the 1980s, reject the system they have and know for the only "other" they have heard about, namely socialism.

Not the least irony of Soviet history flows from the fact that successive leaderships shut down debate among alternative concepts, definitions, and visions of socialism in favor of one official version. Thus, when a crisis of their system arose in 1989, most Soviet citizens did not think they had multiple choices about alternative systems. So Russia "returned" to private capitalism, undoing the 72 years of the Soviet state capitalism that had been officially designated as "socialism" since Stalin.

In that return to date, a mostly state capitalism reverted to a mostly private capitalism. Their common employer/employee structures remained largely intact. The *who* of the employer class went back to private individuals from state officials. A strong central state apparatus regulated that private capitalism. The long isolation of the USSR before and after World War II reinforced an unbalanced economy. Gas and oil were increasingly important exports, while food and manufactured consumer goods often became important imports. Post-1989 Russia has been much less the world's second superpower than it had been as the USSR.

For a world that had largely equated socialism with the USSR for decades, the 1989 implosion of the USSR and its Eastern European allies seemed to mark the "end" of socialism. A kind of capitalist triumphalism coupled itself to a debt-driven neoliberal surge of capitalism in declaring socialism (and communism as well) dead and buried.

Of course, dissenting socialists of various sorts argued that the demise of the USSR was, at most, the end of one interpretation of socialism (and some argued it never was socialism). But such arguments were all but drowned out by capitalists' self-congratulatory triumphalism. Then the 2008 global capitalist crash changed all that.

The demise of the USSR also shook all socialists; it still does. The world's first national, long-lasting experiment in constructing a socialist economy and society collapsed. Its achievements and failures have to be examined to improve socialism's future and especially to enable a more effective socialist intervention when capitalism's contradictions create new opportunities. China's communists have been drawing and applying lessons from the rise and fall of the USSR since the latter's beginning. Indeed, lessons have likewise to be drawn from the rise and fall of the USSR to enable socialists to evaluate that other major new experiment in constructing a socialist society: China.

The People's Republic of China (PRC)

Alliances between the USSR and the eventual Communist Party leaders of the PRC reach back into the 1920s, continued until 1960, rose and fell thereafter, and have recently resumed. There have been strong similarities and solidarities but also deep differences. China entered the 20th century extremely poor, with extreme economic, political, and cultural inequality. While China had resisted Western colonialism sufficiently to remain united, it had suffered deeply humiliating demands, including the establishment of certain Western colonial enclaves (such as Hong Kong) on China's territory. Colonialism's military superiority enforced those demands. The humiliation was and remains informed by a long history that included centuries of a far more advanced Chinese civilization than had then been achieved in Europe. A deep sense of having been overtaken and surpassed by others settled into China's self-consciousness. That continues to fuel a drive for China in turn to overtake and surpass. In a profound sense, socialism (China's version of Soviet-style state capitalism) is seen in China as the proven way to do that.

At the very beginning of the 20th century, the Boxer Rebellion and then the formation of the new republic, with Sun Yat-sen as president, inaugurated a key break from China's past. Feudalisms of various sorts and individual (family) peasant self-employment had been the dominant organizations of workplaces. But a transition to capitalist organizations (employers/employees) was underway. It was increasingly encouraged as a way to catch up with the West and so enable that mix of anti-colonialism and modernization that Chinese leaders (ideological as well as political) championed. As elsewhere, early capitalism produced extreme exploitation on the job and extremely poor living conditions off the job. For just that reason, an early influence of the then-new USSR was to encourage and support anti-capitalist organization among China's new industrial proletariat.

Small early victories led to large defeats for these organizations. Their leaders, especially Mao Zedong, took followers into a kind of distant, internal rural exile to escape slaughter by a military then closely allied to the emerging Chinese capitalism. There, they solidified their organization, undertook an intensive self-education in socialism and especially its Marxian formulations, and studied the history of the USSR. On the basis of those activities they reorganized the local peasant economy in ways that celebrated peasants' collective self-management of farming. They also organized a peasant army.

When Japan invaded China and took over Manchuria in 1931, Chinese society mobilized in self-defense. In the war that lasted basically until 1945, the civil conflict between the dominant capitalist forces (around General Chiang Kai-shek) and the Communist Party resistance (around Mao Zedong and his Eighth Route Army) was suspended. A combined counteroffensive against the Japanese ended with victory and Japanese expulsion in 1945. Immediately a civil war erupted. It ended in 1949 with the complete victory of the Chinese Communist Party. The capitalist forces and army went into exile on the small offshore island of Taiwan. It broke away from the Chinese mainland and is now effectively an independent country with a capitalist economic system.

With its victory in 1949, China's Communist Party leadership faced much the same set of questions as those confronting Lenin in the USSR in 1917. How exactly is the inherited capitalist system to be transformed? What steps are to be taken and in what order, given the goal but also given the obstacles? What parts of the Soviet experience should be replicated and what parts avoided?

Like the USSR, China nationalized capitalist industry, establishing the state as employer and hiring employees to work. Like the USSR, China prioritized industry. China was, with a notable exception, wary of the Soviet experience in agriculture and so more careful in how it responded to peasants' deeply ingrained land hunger. An attempt to rapidly transform agriculture and industrialize (rural commune formation in the 1950s and the Great Leap Forward from 1958-1962) included serious reverses in China's development and major losses and suffering from famine. Consequent policy shifts slowed China's efforts to collectivize, put greater reliance on village government and solidarity to group farmers, led to more balanced investments in industry and agriculture, and so on. China thereby suffered less trauma

78

flowing from its agricultural collectivization efforts than plagued Soviet development after 1929/30.

Like the USSR, China after 1949 confronted political and military dangers from abroad. The Korean War (1950-1953) demonstrated the risks in, for example, the massive bombing of North Korea (mostly by US planes). The Chinese also confronted the fact of the US dropping nuclear bombs on Japan earlier. The result was that Chinese economic development required the use of a major part of its surplus to support a large military apparatus. The early years after 1949 also saw the US refusing to recognize the communist government in Beijing and periodically threatening increased military support for Taiwan's ongoing threat to "retake" the mainland.

The 1960s were years of separation from the USSR as China began to diverge from the Soviet strategy, partly because of its assessment of that strategy. Reduced reliance on the USSR forced a new direction in China's engagement with the rest of the world, especially economically. The formal establishment of US-China diplomatic relations in 1979 marks a further transition from the initial construction of a modern Chinese economy and society to a second stage of rapid economic growth since then. By 1979 China had established its growing importance in the world, its political and ideological independence from the USSR, and its willingness to engage with private capitalism both abroad and inside China.

In broad brush strokes, China's strategy offered an opening for both foreign and domestic private capitalism to find secure places for profitable business inside socialist China. Chinese authorities proposed a kind of basic deal. Private capitalists (foreign, domestic, or partnerships between them) would provide access to capital, modern technology, and foreign markets. Chinese authorities would provide access to skilled, disciplined, and relatively low-cost workers and access to a very large and fast-growing domestic Chinese consumer market. Private enterprises could generate profits that would be shared between them and the Chinese state's taxation system. The Chinese state would closely monitor and supervise all activities by such foreign and domestic enterprises. Their owners and top executives, if Chinese, could also become members of the Chinese Communist Party. Finally, the Chinese state would retain a sizable sector of state-owned and -operated enterprises, and would encourage multilevel partnerships and other relationships among them and private capitalist enterprises, foreign and domestic.

The Chinese state made clear that maximum economic growth focused on industrialization was the overriding objective of its strategy. In that, it was like the USSR. But in its eager embrace of a supervised position for private foreign and domestic capitalism inside Chinese industry, it was very unlike the USSR. The Chinese strategy would have been politically untenable for the USSR for most of its history — perhaps a consequence of being the first socialist experiment to endure. And the Soviet leadership perhaps believed that a more self-contained economic drive to industrialize was a safer route to take.

Given recent claims, a further point is necessary concerning this deal that the PRC offered private capitalists around the world and in China. It was very much a deal meant to be mutually attractive to both sides. Neither side could have coerced the other because neither side had the means to do so. It had to be voluntary and for mutual benefit. Private capitalists invested their capital, shared their technology, and provided access to their customer base to their Chinese partners (private capitalists and/or Chinese state-owned enterprises). They did so because it profited them. For that reason, foreign private capitalism's position in the Chinese economy grew quickly over recent decades. China provided access to its labor force and markets in exchange, an exchange that grew because it benefited both sides.

The Chinese government reported average annual growth rates for its GDP of 10 percent from 1978 to 2005. For the years since then, the widely respected, independent economic consultancy, McKinsey and Company, estimates the growth of China's GDP at annual rates around 10-15 percent from 2005-2010 and then slowly declining to around 6 percent per year in 2019. The International Labour Office similarly reports that average real wages in China rose over 8 percent annually for the decade prior to 2018. Going back further and assembling data from various sources suggests that average Chinese workers' real wages have doubled or tripled at least since 1990. Together with a vast range of statistics, these numbers show that the PRC has been the fastest-growing economy in the world for some decades now. That explains its becoming the number-two economic power in the world after the US and its closing that gap with the US.

In the 20th century, the USSR was the fastest-growing economy; in the 21st century to date the PRC has played that role. Their two kinds of socialism, as they called their economic

81

systems, were alike in achieving extraordinary rates of economic growth and rising real wage/consumption levels. Both countries' governments controlled their banking systems and thus provided ready credits to lubricate their development projects and achieve their growth goals.

China rejected Soviet-type autarchy (adopted by the USSR in the context of global hostility after 1917) in favor of a determined openness to foreign trade and investment. In effect, China planned to industrialize via state and private capitalisms focused on exports. Its low-wage workers would offer profit opportunities to capitalist competitors around the world. China's powerful government would organize and guarantee a basic deal with global capitalists: China will provide cheap labor, government support, and a growing Chinese market in exchange for foreign capitalists partnering with Chinese state or private capitalists, providing their partners with access to technology, and helping Chinese output to enter the wholesale and retail trade systems around the world.

Like the USSR, the People's Republic of China mixed state and private capitalism to achieve rapid economic development. To varying degrees, in both countries, the price paid included deferred consumption, limited civil liberties and freedoms, and no democratic transformation of workplaces. The broader notion of socialism — a system that went beyond economics to include politics and culture — was given a back seat. While both countries experienced rapid economic growth, both also experienced underdeveloped consumption, civil liberties, and personal freedoms.

Anti-socialist argumentation everywhere minimized or simply ignored socialism's rapid economic growth and maximized its relatively low consumption levels, civil liberties, and personal freedoms. Critics' arguments defined socialism as what was actually a state capitalism (state-owned and -operated workplaces replicating private workplaces' employer/employee structure). They depicted socialism as a state/party dictatorship presiding over a failed economy (proven by far lower levels of consumption than in private capitalist economies). Socialism was identified as state and party regimentation of its peoples' political and cultural lives. This message was endlessly pumped into the US landscapes of academia, the mass media, and politics over the last 70 years. Anti-socialists ascribe the 1989 implosion of the USSR to its failed economy, to complete the lessons they draw from the major socialist experiment of the 20th century.

However, somehow the fact is ignored that as capitalism emerged from feudalism in Europe in the 18th and 19th centuries, its advocates promised liberty, equality, fraternity, and democracy. When those promises failed to materialize, the disappointment and anger provoked many to become anti-capitalist and find their way to socialism in the 19th and 20th centuries. That anti-capitalists and then anti-socialists found their ways to parallel criticisms of failures in the systems they opposed raises the possibility that those systems had more in common than their 19th- and 20th-century conflicts saw or admitted.

In contrast, those socialists that engaged in reflective self-criticism before and after 1989 produced a quite different narrative that grounded itself on that commonality and in the failures of both systems. For them, the US and USSR both represented private and state capitalisms whose Cold War enmity was misconstrued on both sides as part of the century's great struggle between capitalism and socialism. In these socialists' view, what collapsed in 1989 was Soviet and Eastern European state capitalism, not socialism. Moreover, what soared after 1989 was another state capitalism in China.

Inside and outside both the USSR and China, many socialists felt that both countries had somehow gotten off track. They had produced societies that were socialist in the old sense of state-owned and -operated workplaces and state planning, but lacked key parts of what socialists had always defined as their goals (equality, solidarity, democracy, and so on). After the 1989 Soviet implosion, a vast process of rethinking and socialist self-criticism set in. It generated a new definition of socialism that pointedly prioritized the micro-level of how workplaces are organized. Socialism is about democratizing workplaces, making them worker cooperatives rather than hierarchical places where small minorities of employers dominate and exclude from major decisions an employee majority.

That new definition informs much of this book, including this chapter's discussion of what happened in the USSR and China. That new definition also generates new goals and a corresponding new strategy for 21st-century socialism. If this new definition strikes readers as unexpected, that is because the anti-socialism campaigns over the last 75 years led many to disconnect from the topic of socialism altogether. Its self-criticism, debates, and changes were, and remain, largely unknown. New socialisms have emerged with newly defined goals and strategies for achieving them.

However, before offering one set of those goals and strategies, we need to explain two other relevant aspects of socialism's modern history (the last century). The first is the "great purge" of socialism led by forces in the United States after World War II and extending, to varying degrees, across the world. The second is fascism, especially in its German Nazi form, a particular kind of state-capitalism merger (that called itself a kind of socialism). Fascists aimed to exterminate the socialist movement and democracy itself from Germany but also from the rest of the world. The mid-20th century's efforts first to exterminate and then to purge socialists had profound social effects that include socialism's changes and current resurgence.

Chapter V

Two Anti-socialist Purges: Fascism and Anti-communism

The 20th century witnessed many repressive attacks on socialism and socialists. They were powerful testimony that socialism — as a critique and alternative to capitalism — was spreading fast and far. Two major anti-socialist purges were accomplished by its enemies. The first was European fascism in the century's first half. The second was US-led global "anti-communism" in the second half. Socialism's various interpretations and changes were profoundly affected by these purges and their social consequences.

"Fascism" is a term that has been applied to many places and times in the social life and history of the 20th century. Here we use it as the name for an economic system, namely capitalism, but with a mixture of very heavy government influence. In fascism, the government reinforces, supports, and sustains private capitalist workplaces — usually because private capitalists fear otherwise losing them, especially during times of social upheaval.

Under fascism, there is a kind of mutually supportive merging of government and private workplaces. Fascist governments tend to "deregulate" worker protections won earlier by unions or socialist governments. They help private capitalists by destroying trade unions or replacing them with their own organizations which support, rather than challenge, private capitalists.

Frequently, fascism embraces extreme nationalism and patriotism to rally people to fascist economic objectives, often by using enhanced military expenditures and hostility toward immigrants or foreigners generally. Fascist governments influence foreign trade to help domestic capitalists sell their goods abroad, and block imports, through tariffs, to help them sell their goods inside national boundaries.

Usually, fascists abhor socialism and promise to save capitalism and the nation from domestic and foreign socialists and communists, treated as threats. In Europe's major fascist systems — Spain under Franco, Germany under Hitler, and Italy under Mussolini — socialists and communists were arrested, imprisoned, and often tortured and killed.

A superficial similarity between fascism and socialism arises because both seek to strengthen government and its interventions into the economy and society. However, they do so in different ways and toward very different ends. Fascism seeks to use the government to secure capitalism and revert to a national unity, defined often in terms of ethnic or religious purity and hierarchy. Socialism seeks to use the government to end capitalism and substitute an alternative socialist economic system, defined traditionally in terms of state-owned and -operated workplaces, state economic planning, employment of dispossessed capitalists, workers' political control, and internationalism.

When fascist leaders took power in Germany in 1933, they had already fought many battles — both in the political arena and in the streets — with socialists in both the German Socialist and Communist parties. Many leading capitalists across the German economy, and many centrist and conservative German politicians, were frightened by the steady growth of the German Socialist Party (SPD) since the 1870s, and by the growth of the German Communist Party (KPD) after World War I.

No one in Germany had any doubts about the extreme right-wing nature and agenda of the Nazi Party and its leader, Adolf Hitler. In the infancy of his Nazi party, Hitler's early decision to adopt the words "socialist" and "workers" into its name (National Socialist German Workers' Party) aimed to draw away some German working-class voters who had overwhelmingly supported the SPD and KPD. In that aim, the Nazis had limited success before 1933, but were then able to draw more support from small-business owners, farmers, unemployed professionals, and religious conservatives. The Nazis had outmaneuvered the traditional, old conservative German parties (discredited by their loss in World War I), to attract many voters and militants.

When the 1929 capitalist crash hit Germany, it was still reeling from its loss in the war. Since 1918, capitalism, and the traditional center-right and right-wing parties supporting it, all suffered rising criticism and popular disdain. German industry saw the political handwriting on the wall. The widespread discontent with the system in power portended the victory of socialists, either those in the SPD, the KPD or both. By 1932, German capitalists saw the Nazis as the only rising mass-based party that could possibly provide broad political support and stem the rising red tide.

So the leading German industrial capitalist association leaned on President von Hindenburg to invite Hitler to form the next German government early in 1933. One of the desired outcomes that this alliance of prominent German capitalists and the Nazis shared was to block, thwart, reduce, and defeat socialism in general, and the SPD and KPD in particular. In the early years of Nazi power, although capitalists supported debilitating the socialist and communist popular movements, in general they did not imagine, let alone understand, that the Nazis could and would exterminate socialists, communists, and many others — physically, and by the millions.

German Nazis were not alone in their persecution of socialists and communists. Europe's other major fascist regimes were also murderous towards socialists, communists, and many of those sympathetic with them. In Spain, Francisco Franco waged a bitter, deadly civil war against the country's elected socialist government and its supporters. Benito Mussolini imposed fascism on Italy for many years, imprisoning and eventually killing the 20th century's greatest Italian socialist leader and theoretician, Antonio Gramsci, as well as many other socialist activists. In Japan, fascists rose to power via the 1931 "Manchurian Incident" to justify their invasion of Manchuria and the 1932 assassination of Prime Minister Inukai Tsuyoshi, which paved the way for Emperor Hirohito's military dictatorship. The savage destruction of Chinese lives and property by Japanese fascism is as well known as its parallels in European fascism's destruction in Europe.

Nazism in Germany was a fascist economic system in which the government lent its support and its force to secure a capitalism that had already been deeply compromised by its pre-World War I alliance with the German kaiser and the German nobility. In this alliance, German capitalists had compromised with feudalism, even as they replaced that system. During the German Empire (1871 - 1918), German capitalists and nobles promoted aggressive competition with British and then US capitalists, and they allied to form an effective bloc against the tide of German socialism that had been rising since the 1870s.

However, that capitalist-feudal alliance (typified by Bismarck and von Hindenburg) was blamed for losing the first world war, for the suffering caused by the war, and then for mismanaging the economic cost of post-war reparations that resulted in the catastrophic 1923 German inflation that wiped out the savings of Germany's middle classes. When the 1929 crash hit, German capitalism tottered. Half the country supported socialists and communists. The other half was split and decreasingly friendly to capitalism. Even fascists called themselves "national socialists" to signal that their right-wing nationalism included a solid dose of anti-capitalism. German capitalists grasped their social vulnerability. They knew all too well what had happened to Russian capitalists only a few years earlier.

In 1932 German Nazism and German capitalism reached an accommodation. Each acquired crucial assistance, and each paid a price for it. The Nazis acquired governmental power via Hitler's ascendancy to his position as the supreme German leader, or *der Führer*. With that power, Nazism acquired the means to increase and strengthen itself while destroying or subordinating all other political parties. Nazis in power thereby also acquired the means to rearm Germany to avenge the loss of the World War and the subsequent humiliations. The price the Nazis paid was losing inside the Nazi movement, through extermination, its explicitly anti-capitalist elements and sympathisers, including Gregor and Otto Strasser, among many others.

The capitalists achieved a mass political base that officially supported and celebrated capitalism and the leading German capitalists (excluding Jews). The capitalists also achieved a government that would oppose and crush all socialist, or even independent, organizations of the working class (unions, social movements, etc.) or convert them into loyal supporters of German fascism. The price capitalists had to pay for Nazi supports was basically a merger or combination between capitalism and Nazism. German fascism assigned to major German capitalists a kind of ongoing, close association with Nazism's top leadership. Capitalists' economic decisions were closely coordinated with Nazi leaders' political decisions. In many cases, where differences arose, the latter prevailed. While there were always some capitalists who rejected or refused to accept the merger, the vast majority did neither.

They accepted the price of the merger and subordination to the Nazi party and government because it was the best, or perhaps even the only, option to preserve German capitalism.

The Nazi government destroyed socialist and independent labor unions and subordinated them instead to the control of German state and Nazi Party officials. The Nazi government destroyed socialist parties and persecuted socialist academics, artists, intellectuals, and activists. Thousands were deported, imprisoned, exiled, killed, or compelled to flee, and Nazi leaders boasted to their capitalist partners that they had eliminated socialism from German life.

The fascist merger of state officials and leading capitalists enabled Germany to escape from reparations-related restrictions imposed after World War I's defeat. Fascism built a German economic recovery after the 1929-1932 crash by reducing unemployment via rapid rearmament. It redesigned European trade patterns to advance German interests. Finally, it undertook systematic planning for the expansion of Germany to form a new German empire.

Germany's turn to fascism raised yet again the broad question of state versus private capitalism. During the 19th and 20th centuries, state versus private capitalism was often debated as the core issue of the overall debate between capitalism and socialism. The political, economic, and social goals of state capitalism were radically different for socialists on the left versus fascists on the right. But many discussions focused solely on state capitalism's existence and differences from private capitalism, and lost sight of different state capitalisms' profoundly different goals and purposes.

This is part of a larger issue of confusing state capitalism with socialism. When state capitalism happened, capitalism was instead said to have given way to socialism. When private capitalism was threatened by government encroachments via regulations, taxations, or nationalized workplaces, it was said that socialism was threatening or overtaking capitalism. When states privatized state-owned and -operated workplaces or deregulated them or cut their tax obligations, it was often done by "conservative" politicians. They said they were reviving or returning to capitalism and getting rid of socialism or socialist elements in their societies.

Similar confusing transitions occurred during the declining phases of the slave and feudal economic systems: from relatively decentered, private forms to concentrated, centralized state forms. Deepening problems of maintaining slave economies (i.e., economies where production was organized around masters and slaves) provoked private masters eventually to solve those problems by making or permitting a state apparatus that was itself a master with slaves. In short, a co-existing and specifically empowered state slavery proved to be one way to sustain private slavery. Much the same evolution happened as private feudal manors produced the absolute feudal states during late European feudalism.

The co-existence of state and private slavery or of state and private feudalism was rarely achieved peacefully. Disagreements among private slave masters over establishing that co-existence, and anxieties among and between private and state slave masters over managing that co-existence, could and did lead to conflicts. These included violent clashes. Again, a similar history attended European feudalism.

However, the co-existence of their private and state forms does not warrant thinking that those systems were not slave or feudal, and so it is the same with the confusion of state capitalism and socialism. The Nazis were not socialists (even with the word "socialist" in their name), and the heavy hand of the Nazi party created a fascist state capitalism, not socialism. In contrast, modern capitalism has debated to exhaustion whether state forms of its employer/employee structure mean capitalism is threatened, dying, or passing over into a different economic system — socialism. The co-existence of state and private forms of capitalism are rather like parallel co-existences in slavery and feudalism.

Indeed, the relatively faster growth of state-capitalist forms may parallel slavery and feudalism in yet another way. Those systems secured their reproduction in part by means of transitioning from decentralized, minimal state institutions to powerfully centralized state institutions embodying state forms of master/slave and lord/serf production structures. Perhaps the last century entails capitalism entering a similar transition from decentralized private to centralized state forms, but with this peculiarity: The transition was misperceived as a change of system itself rather than a change between forms of the same system.

Nazis understood themselves as the means to save German capitalism, as part of the German nation, from its leftist critics (lumped together under the term "bolshevism"). The close, ongoing collaborations between the Nazi state and leading

German capitalists exceeded anything that had happened in the history of German capitalism before that. There were striking similarities between German fascism and the previous close alliance of the Prussian state with leading feudal lords in the regions that later became modern Germany.

The Nazis repressed socialists systematically after January 1933, including eventually their wholesale murder, imprisonment, drafting into the German military, and deportation. Those who survived and remained went underground. Elsewhere across Europe, where Nazi Germany ruled, the repression of socialism was likewise harsh. This was also the case among Nazi Germany's allies in Italy, Spain, and beyond. In Spain, for example, Franco's fascism decimated the ranks of young socialists for decades, not only in Spain but also in the many countries that sent brilliant young volunteers to fight in the 1930s Spanish Civil War. Young people growing up inside fascism learned a lasting lesson in the immense risks taken by individuals drawn to socialist theory and practice. At the same time, a socialist underground developed both ideologically and organizationally. Underground socialist solidarity proved a strong basis for European socialism's revival after 1945.

The impact of fascism on socialism took multiple forms. One that is particularly important concerns fascism's impact on the relative strengths of different interpretations or different tendencies or traditions within socialism. After 1917, the success of the socialist revolutionaries in Russia gave their interpretation of socialism the prestige of having achieved the first enduring governmental position for socialists. In the 1920s and 1930s, Soviet socialism had to contend with criticisms from other socialists. Communists debated and contended with socialists. Other socialists contested the prestige and relative strength of the international communist tradition. Fascism renewed the exceptional prestige and strength of Soviet socialism.

This happened for two main reasons. First, local communists were connected via the Communist International, or *Comintern*. This was an international organization of communists who collaborated with one another to share lessons learned, coordinate strategies, etc. The USSR was its effective leader. Since the USSR was the Nazis' main target and enemy, Nazi occupations targeted local communists more harshly than other socialists. Communists went underground sooner and developed better underground linkages. For these and other reasons, communists rose to leadership positions in many underground resistance movements against fascism across Europe. Experiences there strengthened their solidarity, prestige, and support relative to other socialists, and their ability to advance politically after fascism was defeated.

Second, the USSR prevented the Nazi invasion from overthrowing Soviet socialism and then drove fascist forces from their territory and across Eastern Europe all the way to Berlin. That reinforced the prestige and power of the Soviet brand of socialism once again. In this remarkable way, fascism worked ultimately to strengthen Soviet socialism despite the massive physical damage done to the Soviet people and economy by fascist military forces.

Already toward the end of World War II, the USSR and the US anticipated, and were planning for, their likely split and transformation from victorious allies into rivals. As it happened, they quickly went beyond rivalry to an enmity of Cold War proportions. The much greater wealth of the US, its atomic bomb and global military reach, and fear of how the Soviet government might use its enhanced post-war political strength gave the US a dominant position in the world after 1945. The US used that position to design and unleash a global program of systematic anti-communism targeting the USSR and the influence of communists linked to it. (The Truman Doctrine was a policy epitomizing the "containment" of communism.)

The 20th century's second major purge of socialism thus got underway and has continued at varying levels of intensity ever since. It represented the replacement of fascism's purging of socialism led by Germany with what might be called a centrist purge led by the US. Capitalism's global crash in 1929 led to greater interest in socialism in both countries, which in turn also led to reactions against a rising socialism: German-led fascism in one instance, US-led anti-communism in another.

The reaction to the 1930s Great Depression in the US differed from that in Germany. While both sets of working classes developed strong anti-capitalist views and many moved toward socialism, fascist reactions in the US were much weaker and much less well organized than in Germany. Franklin D. Roosevelt (FDR) proved a very different leader from Hitler. An alliance of parts of the US's Democratic Party, Communist Party, two socialist parties, and a surging labor movement (Congress of Industrial Organizations, or CIO) comprised the New Deal coalition. It was the mass base for FDR's progressive laws, multiple re-elections, and resolute anti-fascism. US socialists obtained from FDR's government a degree of social acceptance, stature, and support never before accorded them. The wartime alliance of the US with the USSR strengthened that social acceptance and socialist influences.

One result of those influences was the government tax and spending policies of the 1930s and 1940s. In short, FDR's government taxed the rich more than ever before and used the money to provide mass public services more than ever before. FDR established the Social Security system, the first federal unemployment compensation system, the first federal minimum wage, and a mass federal jobs program, among other government-supported social programs.

FDR raised the revenue necessary for Washington to fund such public services in the depths of the 1930s Depression. He likewise raised revenues to finance the US role in World War II. He did so by taxing corporations and the rich. He also borrowed from them. Nevertheless, FDR's attack on wealth and privilege to fund jobs and services for the poor and middle income citizens did not destroy his political position as critics and enemies had threatened. Quite the opposite. FDR was re-elected three times, and was arguably the most popular president in US history. He was also the president most pushed politically from below by a coalition of communists, socialists, and unionists. He had been no radical Democrat before his election.

Massive government intervention to redistribute wealth, income, and government support from corporations and the rich to average citizens reflected the unprecedented political power of the US left. That reality — and especially the power of the New Deal coalition — drove a commitment among private capitalists and the Republican Party to undo the New Deal. The end of World War II and FDR's death in 1945 provided the right time and circumstances to destroy the New Deal coalition.

The specific target for this project became a massive purging of socialist influences. In this way, the coalition that had produced FDR's New Deal could be broken. Anti-communism quickly became the battering ram with which to do that. Overnight, the USSR went from close ally to demon enemy, whose agents were everywhere in communist parties operating as arms of an effort "to control the world." This threat had to be contained, repelled, eliminated.

In the US, Communist Party leaders were arrested, imprisoned, and deported, in a wave of anti-communism that quickly spread to socialist parties and to socialism in general. Sequentially, "communism," "socialism," "Marxism," "totalitarianism," and "anarchism" became *de facto* synonyms — lumped together by the general concept of "anti-communism." Any and all of these practices had to be driven back and out of the US and the rest of the world as far as possible. Domestic and foreign policy of the United States became centrally focused on anti-communism. Because the US after 1945 had the world's largest economy and most powerful military, it also wielded the dominant political-power position. Hence it held the central position in crafting the United Nations, World Bank, the International Monetary Fund, NATO, and so on. Once the US committed itself to total anti-communism, its allies and most of the rest of the world followed suit more or less as their domestic situations enabled or allowed.

The Chinese Revolution's success under Mao's leadership a few years after the end of World War II provoked even more heightened anti-communism. It reached hysterical dimensions culminating in the public campaigns of US Senator Joseph McCarthy. "McCarthyism" became a general label attached to such political hysterias. In the US, key moments and forms marked the excoriation of communists (and usually likewise of many socialists, especially if they had been open about their ideological commitments). In 1947, the Taft-Hartley Act prevented Communist Party members from holding union leadership positions (whether or not union members had voted them into those positions). Most US unions went further and removed socialists from leadership positions, expelled or took over locals thought to be controlled by socialists, and generally sent all union members a basic memo: Keep away from socialism and socialists (regardless of their specific labels, such as communist, anarchist, leftist, etc.).

Hollywood actors, directors, screenwriters, musicians, and more were blacklisted and barred from working in the industry, effectively destroying the careers of hundreds of working professionals, and thus ensuring American popular media would be unsympathetic to socialism. The war in Korea was presented as emblematic of the new international polarization. On one side was the "West, " portrayed as capitalistic, free, democratic, and good. On the other was the "East," the opposite place demonized as socialistic, totalitarian, and bad. Educators — from elementary school teachers through college and university professors — got fired, demoted, and/or otherwise disciplined if they taught, spoke, or wrote otherwise. Suddenly many professors with strong or weak sympathies for socialist critiques of capitalism found that their work could no longer get published, that colleagues stopped assigning their work as required reading for students, that invitations to present their work at scholarly conferences dried up. The teaching profession received the same message that had swept across the unions, Hollywood, and the American public in general. The number-one enemy of the US was now socialism, communism, and the Soviet "evil empire."

Around the world, US foreign policy likewise targeted socialism. Sometimes the label was applied to persons, groups, organizations, and movements that were self-defined as socialist. At other times, political struggles abroad competed for US government support by branding their enemies as socialists. Then too, profit-driven struggles among business groups, or between them and government officials, led them to seek US support by accusing their adversaries of being "socialist." Examples include US policies and actions especially in Guatemala and Iran (1954), Cuba (1959-1961), Vietnam (1954-1975), South Africa (1945-1994), Venezuela (since 1999), among many, many others.

Anti-communism was likewise the central theme and focus of US military policies in the post-1945 nuclear age. The US established a ring of thousands of military bases surrounding the USSR, then Soviet allies in Eastern Europe, then China, and so on. The US contested political groupings in Asia, Africa, and Latin American countries seen to be socialist. Inside allied

European countries, it helped repress socialist officials, groups, and parties in favor of their opponents.

The US government found or established allies to assist its international anti-communism. Where US officials found anti-communist organizations in a country, they helped establish, build, and/or fund them. Where such organizations already existed but were weak, US officials helped or supplemented them. These included church and missionary groups, business associations, individual corporations, and labor unions. The US foreign-policy establishment included the leadership of the AFL-CIO. Academic associations and individual professors were recruited and funded (overtly and covertly) by the US government or its allies to produce research that would advance the anti-communist project.

Sometimes, regime change was the form taken by the global anti-communism project, when and where local conditions made that possible. Early in the post-World War II period, Iran's Mossadegh fell victim, as did Guatemala's Árbenz. In 1965-6 the mass killings of Indonesian communists were estimated to cost the lives of 500,000 to three million. Shortly after the 1959 victory of Cuba's revolution, the new Castro government faced overt opposition from the US, then an embargo and an armed effort to overthrow that government directed and supported by the US. The overthrow effort was defeated, but Cuba was thereafter isolated. Anti-communism was the major theme and preoccupation of US policies in and for Latin America for the subsequent decades. Many more examples exist, culminating in the undercutting of the USSR and its Eastern European allied governments. Each instance had its unique characteristics. However, the presence and effectiveness of the US-led global anti-communism project were always important contributors of a particular context for each local struggle.

Nearly everywhere, socialists, communists, and their organizations were undermined, repressed, or outright destroyed. The progress of socialism that had so frightened capitalism's supporters before, during, and in the aftermath of fascism was slowed by US-led global anti-communism. The demise of the USSR and Eastern European socialist governments especially raised the triumphalist idea that perhaps anti-communism had succeeded beyond its hopes. Perhaps the 20th century's struggle between capitalism and socialism/communism had been definitively decided in the former's favor. Amid a surging global neoliberalism — as the post-1970s successor to the previously (1930s-1970s) dominant Keynesianism — post-communism seemed assured.

However, the 2008 global crash reminded many millions that capitalism was its own worst enemy. As hundreds of millions lost jobs, incomes, homes, and savings, socialist criticisms of capitalism resurfaced and captured new generations' loyalties. Once again, capitalism's tendencies toward inequality, instability, and injustice became common knowledge. The capitalist triumphalism that had soared since 1989 faded quickly. For the first time in 70 years, a candidate for the US presidency could accept the label "socialist" and do far, far better in getting votes than anyone had foreseen. Thereafter, hundreds of US socialists are seeking political office, and increasing numbers are winning.

Socialist criticisms of Soviet and Chinese socialisms and of European social democracy reflected a growing range of debates within and about socialism. The socialist tradition's pre-1917 diversity of interpretations and tendencies — and lively debates around them — began to resurface. The populisms provoked by rejections of neoliberalism and its old politics (oscillating center-right and center-left parties) generated a new socialist left. Old socialist parties shrank, disappeared, or changed leadership in the face of new anti-capitalist parties and mass movements (such as Podemos in Spain, Syriza in Greece, the "yellow vests" in France, Corbyn-type leadership in the UK's Labour Party, and so on).

Socialist anti-capitalism began to reappear explicitly in the mass media, in school curricula, and in politics. Traditional politicians increasingly attacked socialism where before they had ignored its existence or treated it as some long-dead historic relic. Environmental activists found ready allies in the rebounding socialism as did a new generation of labor-union militants. Where before activists on issues of race, gender, and other progressive movements had carefully avoided economic issues in general and socialist approaches in particular, after 2008 their coalitions with socialists became easier to negotiate and manage. Thus in 2011 the "Occupy Wall Street" movement made its slogan of the one percent versus the 99 percent a centerpiece of its global movement. The welcome openness to a socialist trope was obvious.

The 20th century's two great purges of socialism had failed to bury it or stop its development. They had, however, slowed it and left deep traces. Two or more generations had been traumatized: History had shown them that socialist thoughts and actions were extremely dangerous and costly on a personal level. Given pro-capitalist ideologies' influences, many young people turned away from political engagement. Individual effort, focus, and achievement took precedence and absorbed energies. Workers' response to the exhaustion and injustices of the workplace focused chiefly on consumption, as all advertising urged. Buying was the appropriate and adequate compensation for alienating labor. In the worker's day, the "happy hours" began immediately after work in the bar and then later at the mall. Struggling to improve work conditions (and therefore learning and mastering the associated socialist theories and practices) fell out of fashion. They seemed less attractive and less effective.

Socialism was hurt, but also taught, by the two great purges it suffered. Defeats and sharp criticisms sent many of its best thinkers to return to fundamentals, to ask hard, critical questions, and produce new tendencies within socialist thought. With active socialism dangerously repressed, many socialists redirected their energies to other social movements (anti-racism, feminism, ecology, and so on), giving them a stronger socialist component. Likewise, that served to bring all sorts of important insights and arguments developed in and by those social movements into socialist consciousness, debates, and development. Socialists rediscovered that it is never repression itself, but rather how a repressed movement copes with repression, that determines its ultimate effects. Socialism's history since 1945 has seen ups and downs, declines and resurgences. Out of its evaluations of the two great experiments in the USSR and the PRC, its responses to criticisms and repression, and the endless provocations of capitalism and its failures, socialism has made major changes and emerged in the 21st century with renewed power and influence.

The two great purges of the 20th century did not settle the struggle between capitalism and socialism. The 21st century's first two decades have shown the struggle is very much alive and ongoing. As socialism changed profoundly in the transition from the 19th to the 20th century, so it did again a century later. Its shifting nature, composition, and trajectory give every sign of shaping the 21st century too.

Chapter VI

Socialism's Future and Worker Co-ops

In this book's Introduction we referred to socialism as a yearning for something better than capitalism. As capitalism has changed and as experiments with socialism have accumulated — both good and bad — socialist yearnings, too, have changed. However, a bizarre disconnect surfaces as capitalism's gross dysfunction during and since its 2008 crash brings socialism again into public discussion. Large numbers of people debate the pros and cons of socialism as if what it is in the 21st century were identical to what it was in the 20th. Is it reasonable to presume that the last century's two purges, the Cold War, the implosion of the USSR, and the explosive emergence of the People's Republic of China inspired no critical reflections on socialism by socialists themselves? No. The remarkable lack of awareness of new and different definitions of socialism since 1945, their elaborations, and their implications reflects the fact that sustained engagement with socialism was taboo in the US for decades. That people are now mostly unaware of socialism's evolution in theory, practice, and self-criticism over the last half century is therefore no surprise.

The taboo against socialism resulted in a mass retreat from engaging with developments in socialism and connecting these developments to the problems of modern capitalism. Socialism rather became one of two things in the minds of most.

On the one hand, many politicians, academics, and media pundits portrayed socialism as coinciding with Soviet efforts to subvert global capitalism. Socialism for such people meant moving from private to state-owned and -operated workplaces and from market to centrally planned distributions of resources and products. These same people equated opposing capitalism with opposing democracy and freedom. This equation was then repeated endlessly in an effort to make it "common sense."

On the other hand, socialism was the name adopted by Western European — and especially Scandinavian — "welfare-state" governments, which aimed to regulate markets comprised still mostly of private capitalist firms. This led many people to associate socialism with robust public spending and government intervention in the marketplace.

Consequently, socialism was viewed as more or less extreme, depending on whether it involved state-owned and -operated firms with central planning at one end or merely welfare-state policies with market regulation on the other. The words "communist" and "socialist" sometimes designated the more and less extreme versions, respectively.

As a result of these wooden definitions of socialism, its evolution and diversity were obscured. Socialists themselves were struggling with what they viewed as the mixed results of the first major, enduring experiments in constructing socialist societies (USSR, PRC, Cuba, Vietnam, etc.). To be sure, these socialist experiments achieved remarkable and admirable economic growth. Such growth enabled mutual assistance among socialist societies, which was crucial to their defense and survival. Socialism thereby established itself globally as capitalism's chief rival and likely successor. In the Global South, socialism arose virtually everywhere as the alternative development model to a capitalism weighed down by its colonialist history and its contemporary problems of inequality, instability, and injustice.

Yet socialists also struggled with some negative aspects of these first experiments in socialism, particularly the emergence of strong central governments that often used their concentrated economic power to achieve political dominance in very undemocratic ways. Many socialists agreed with critical denunciations of political dictatorship, even though some of these criticisms ignored the parallel dictatorships within capitalist megacorporations. Struggles of workers in socialist societies against internal exploitation and oppression likewise affected socialists' thinking. Some socialist theorists — for instance, Milovan Djilas and his circle in the non-Soviet socialist republic of Yugoslavia — began to apply class analysis to Soviet-type socialisms, and argued that party bureaucrats were a new class. One implication of this line of thought was that the USSR had not broken from class anywhere near as thoroughly as it had proclaimed. Whatever the pronouncements of party leaders and apologists, many socialists after 1945, and even more after 1989, grasped the unfinished, incomplete, and inadequate state of the socialist projects of their day.

Such socialist dissenters made various efforts to "open the windows" of the musty atmosphere within official circles of socialism after 1945. (These words came from an impassioned member of the French Communist Party, Étienne Balibar, and echoed the critical theoretical stance of his teacher, Louis Althusser.) Young socialists during the globally widespread protests of 1968 asked new and different questions of an older generation of socialists. Eurocommunism sought some kind of compromise between the communist type of socialism in the Soviet bloc and the social-democratic type in Western Europe. Strains of anarchist thought and practice returned as possible ways to advance socialist ideals without the fraught statism that had been associated with these ideals. Maoist communes emerged as another possible way to advance these ideals, as was the case with Yugoslav cooperatives and Israeli *kibbutzim* earlier.

Socialists over the last half century were also profoundly shaken by criticisms from emerging social movements on the left. Anti-racists, feminists, and environmentalists — many of whom had started in socialist circles — began to criticize socialists for disregarding or minimizing the primary foci of their struggles. Socialist feminism and eco-socialisms, for example, sought to take these criticisms to heart. Likewise, socialists everywhere began to rethink what a socialist position ought to emphasize in order to integrate the demands and goals of social movements with which it sought alliances.

One strain of somewhat superficial socialist self-criticism stressed socialism's inadequate recognition and institutionalization of democracy. This self-criticism acknowledged and accommodated socialism's critics, many of whom asserted the absence of political democracy in socialist societies. Such thinking also sharpened the struggle within socialism between communist tendencies and social-democratic tendencies. The latter usually functioned within parliamentary systems, where socialists — even when they held elected power — had to govern democratically. These social democrats advertised their democratic credentials against socialists from countries where communist parties ruled. Thus, when Eastern European socialist regimes dissolved after 1989, many socialists in these countries sought transitions to Western European-type socialisms. In some cases — for instance, in Hungary and Poland — their hopes were badly disappointed. [6]

Socialists who called for political democracy to be added to the socialist economic system confronted several questions and problems. First, how is that to be done? Merely adding multiple political parties and elections was surely not the answer. Socialists knew better than most how wealth, income, and economic power tended to concentrate in capitalist corporate hands, thereby rendering parties and elections formalities with little democratic substance. Why should socialists think that parallel concentrations in state-owned and -operated workplaces would yield a different outcome?

A larger problem for the project of merging socialism with democracy concerned the question of where such a merger was to occur. Was democracy to be located in relations between the state, individual workplaces, and individual citizens; between different people inside workplaces; or in both? Would workplaces be counted like individuals in liberal democracies: one vote each, regardless of wealth, size, and so on? Would democracy be institutionalized inside every workplace so that all employees, with one vote each, could decide democratically what, how, and where the workplace produces and what is done with output and revenues? If so, how would such workplace democracy interact in a democratic manner with those affected outside a given workplace — for instance, customers or others in the surrounding communities? Capitalism never faced, let alone solved, these problems, so figuring out how socialism might do so proved difficult for the socialists who undertook the task.

For many socialists, such questions and problems proved too demanding. Such socialists resorted to abstract invocations of democracy with little or no attention to the specifics. Anti-socialists could continue to berate the shrinking number of communist-party-led societies for their absence of democratic forms (pretending, as usual, that the forms equaled the substance of democracy). Meanwhile, avowed socialists, like Sanders in the US or Corbyn in the UK, pointed to Western European-type socialisms as proof of the merits of "democratic socialism."

Increasingly after the 2008 crash of capitalism, however, many socialists grasped the deeper issue of inadequate and incomplete democracy, both in conventional socialisms and in capitalisms, whether private or state. To invoke transition from communism to capitalism in the name of democracy — as was widely done before and even more so after 1989 — was to demote democracy from substance to formality. What struck growing numbers of socialists was that the absence of real, substantial democracy had undermined both traditional capitalisms and traditional socialisms. In the former, collaboration of the wealthiest and most powerful private capitalists with the state apparatus resulted in an undemocratic social and political oligarchy. In the latter, collaboration of the wealthiest and most powerful state and private economic enterprises with the state political apparatus resulted in much the same.

The effort to incorporate democracy into socialist frameworks taught those engaged in the project that the same task applied to capitalism. Systemic differences had blinded the 20th century to some basic similarities between capitalism and conventional socialisms. One key similarity is the internal structure or organization of workplaces and the related nature of the relationship between workplaces and the state. In both systems — recognizing all their variations — workplaces are organized in a starkly undemocratic manner. As socialists moved toward democratizing workplaces, socialism itself changed, resulting in the emergence of a major new socialist tendency at the close of the 20th century.

In both private and state capitalisms ("actually existing socialisms"), workplaces display a basic dichotomy between employers and employees. In private capitalisms, the employers are not typically members of any state apparatus. Except in the smallest of workplaces, employers are rather a small minority of individuals engaged at the workplace. This minority makes all the key workplace decisions, including what to produce, how, and where, and what should be done with the output. The majority — employees hired by the employers — are excluded from making such decisions but are nonetheless required to accept and live with them. In private capitalisms, employees can quit an employer, but that normally requires them to enter another workplace organized in the same way.

In actually existing socialisms, state-regulated or state-owned and -operated workplaces display this same dichotomy, or split. A small minority — in this case, employers who are private citizens or state officials — hires the majority, namely the employees who do most of the work. The minority similarly excludes the majority from key workplace decisions.

In relationships between the state and workplaces, the employers, whether private owners or state officials, are the intermediaries that "represent" the workplace. The employees play a secondary role or no role at all in this relationship. Outside the workplace, the mass of employees, as citizens, might periodically elect a candidate to office, but it is these politicians who subsequently enter state-workplace relationships with employers, whether the latter be private proprietors or state officials like themselves. The structure of this relationship serves to keep most employees removed from all but occasional, marginal influences on economic events and curtails any real economic democracy.

Through these lessons, a growing number of socialists have come to focus on worker cooperatives as a means to achieve tangible economic democracy. Such socialists reject master/slave, lord/serf, and employer/employee relationships because these all preclude real democracy. Socialist proponents of worker cooperatives seek to construct alternative workplaces that specifically avoid all such dichotomies. They do so in the name of ending the inequalities these dichotomies have always fostered and promoting the democracy such dichotomies have always refused. The goal is a transition away from all employer/employee workplace organizations toward those in which employees are also — simultaneously and collectively — employers. This new kind of socialism thus champions worker cooperatives where workers function democratically as their own employers.

Such ideas and aspirations are not new. They have existed and circulated among slaves, serfs, and workers who yearned for something better across the centuries. Collective workplaces where workers directed themselves, often democratically, existed in previous times and places. For example, individual serfs and village communes sometimes organized workplaces in democratic ways within European feudal societies. So too did craftspersons in some feudal guilds.

Toward the end of the 19th century, especially in France and Spain, labor unions developed programs that went well beyond the confines of collective bargaining with employers over wages and working conditions. In a movement called "syndicalism" (after the French word for "labor union," *syndicat*), workers demanded that labor unions replace capitalist employers entirely so that the employees would become their own employers. Other, anarchist, movements included demands for workers controlling their own workplaces as well.

In short, there were many precursors for the idea and organization of worker cooperatives. For the most part, however, the dominant theory and practice of 19th- and 20th-century socialisms downplayed or marginalized democratized workplaces. Especially following the reverses suffered by late-20th-century socialisms, though, a new 21st-century socialism is busily rediscovering, renewing, and reformulating programs for democratizing workplaces. These programs now give priority and emphasis to worker cooperatives in achieving a transition from capitalism to an alternative, democratic economic order.

In their modern forms, worker co-ops provide all who labor inside a workplace — whether factory, office, or store — with an equal voice on the key business decisions. Majorities determine what, how, and where the workplace produces; how it uses or distributes its outputs; and how it relates to the state. The state's direct partner in its relationship to the workplace is no longer a minority, the employers, but instead the entire collective of employee-owners. By democratizing workplaces, worker co-ops can give shape to a real, daily democracy on a society-wide basis.

Democratized workplaces provide a foundation — an institutional structure, habits of thinking and acting, training, and a model — for a democratic politics in residential communities. In the past, the undemocratic employer/employee relationship of capitalist and socialist societies undermined workers' agency in politics. The very idea of a real political democracy seemed remote, purely imaginary, and vaguely utopian. In contrast, a transition from employer/employee workplace organization in private and state workplaces to an alternative worker co-op organization establishes real democracy in the economic sphere. That in turn offers better prospects for socialists to revitalize demands and movements for a parallel democracy in the political one.

An economy based on worker co-ops would revolutionize the relationship between the state and the people. In their capacity as a self-employed collectivity, workers would occupy the spot traditionally held by the workplace in state-workplace relations and interactions. The former go-between in the state-workplace relationship — the employers — would be subsumed by the collective of worker-owners. The workers would collectively and democratically hold the purse strings to which the state would have to appeal. The state would thus depend on citizens and workers rather than the other way around. The state would depend on *citizens* in the usual residence-based public arena of elections and voting (or their equivalents). The state would also depend on *workers* in the other social arena: state-workplace interactions. In both arenas, real democracy would have taken giant steps forward. The state would no longer pretend to occupy the role of neutral arbiter in struggles between master and slave, lord and serf, employer and employee. The state would have fewer ways and means to impose its own momentum and goals upon citizens or workplaces. To that extent, the state's "withering away" would become more immediately achievable than in any other variety of socialism known thus far.

The democratization of workplaces immediately raises the issue — indeed the necessity — of extending that democratization to the people affected by workplaces who are not workers there. The communities in which workplaces function should have a democratic relationship with these workplaces which, after all, pay taxes to these communities and make decisions that can shape local traffic patterns, air quality, and so on. Such should also be the case with customers and other stakeholders of worker co-ops.

Decisions reached inside democratized workplaces by their workers must be shared with, and co-determined by, democratic decisions of customers and affected localities and regions. Such co-determination would also need to agree upon rules for developing, enforcing, and adjudicating disputes and disagreements. A system of checks and balances among workplaces, residential communities, and consumers would need to be constructed.

The key difference between the emerging socialism of the 21st century and the previous socialist tradition is the former's advocacy of the microeconomic transformation of the internal structure and organization of workplaces. The transition from hierarchical, dichotomous employer/employee organizations of workplaces to worker co-ops grounds a bottom-up economic democracy on a wider, structural level. The new socialism's difference from capitalism becomes less a matter of state versus private workplaces, and state planning versus private markets, and more a matter of democratic versus autocratic workplace organization. A new economy based on worker co-ops will have to find its own democratic way to structure relationships among co-ops and society as a whole. Such an economy will need to work out, for instance, the best proportion of planned versus market distributions, and private versus public workplace ownership, as well as determine the specific structure of laws and regulations. Worker co-ops are thus doing anew what capitalist workplaces did in their emergence from a dying feudalism. In this manner, the new socialism emerges from the practical experiences and experiments of the old, and the theoretical self-criticisms it provoked.

In the new light of such a 21st-century socialism, history looks different. We can see that the kingdoms banished from the public, political sphere survived inside the private space of workplaces. Monarchy and autocracy were not banished completely in the modern era but rather relocated inside workplaces, where democracy was proscribed. These autocratic spaces then provided their owner-monarchs with the means to agitate against democracy in the political sphere. Before the end of political monarchy, conservatives worried that civilization could not survive without the sovereign leadership of the king and his court. Now, before the end of capitalism, conservatives worry that the economy, and thus civilization itself, cannot survive without the leadership of a boss and executives inside workplaces.

In response to this sentiment, profit incentives indeed motivate employers to achieve success in our current economy. But the employer/employee organization of the workplace produces tensions and conflicts that will always yield counterproductive employee motivations. In worker co-ops, employees tend to work harder and better because the enterprise belongs to them, not their employers. In capitalist workplaces, employers and employees struggle over the redistribution of the wealth they produce. Those struggles worsen and embitter social divisions. In worker co-ops, members democratically determine any distribution of work and wealth precisely to prevent and preclude social divisiveness.

A new socialism focused on transforming workplaces into worker co-ops offers a new generation of socialists a particularly effective political strategy. The old tradition of socialism taught its enemies to focus their critical counterattack on socialism's statist tendencies. Those enemies are not prepared, at least not yet, to defend against a socialism defined instead in terms of workplace democratization and employee ownership. This unpreparedness gives socialists a strategic advantage. This new socialism also provides a solid basis on which socialists can critically appreciate and go beyond the old socialist tradition. The new socialism can applaud how the old tradition built up powerful political parties, won power in major countries, and spread interest and awareness of socialism across the globe. Yet it can also confront and overcome the limits of the old tradition, especially its statism, which shifted from being a means of socialism's expansion to being a fetter on it.

Worker co-ops have a long history and a wide presence in today's world. To take one leading example of the many thousands of worker co-ops across the world, the Corporación Mondragon in the Basque region of Spain offers over half a century's experience as proof of the viability of this economic model. Mondragon started with six workers and now includes over 80,000. It is now one of Spain's 10 largest corporations. Throughout its history, it has found ways for small worker co-ops to mature into large ones and even for worker co-ops to win against capitalist competitors within the same industry. Mondragon has shown how worker co-ops can grow while co-existing with capitalist workplaces within one society. Mondragon also offers solid strategies for successful worker co-op relationships and interactions with states. Of course, Mondragon's stunningly successful growth was not without its reverses and rough patches, some of which resulted from wider global factors; capitalism's cyclic instabilities; and the co-op's own missteps, learning issues, and flaws.

Modern societies, both capitalist and socialist, have more than enough shortcomings — i.e., inequalities, instabilities, injustices, lack of real democracy — to enable and provoke their citizens to pursue a promising alternative. The evidence, theoretical and empirical, is here: Worker co-ops *are* that alternative. The needed next step is to build worker co-op sectors across our contemporary societies. That would allow citizens to encounter, work in, and buy from worker co-ops alongside conventional private and state capitalist workplaces. Such a sector would provide the basis for citizens to make informed choices about what mix of alternative workplace organizations work best.

In the UK and the US, socialist political leaders like Jeremy Corbyn and Bernie Sanders advocate governmental support for worker co-ops. This support would entail laws giving employees a right of first refusal when an employer considers certain basic changes in the enterprise. Workers, for instance, might choose to buy an enterprise that would otherwise be sold to another individual or corporation and convert it into a worker co-op. This support would also entail lending workers the initial funds at an affordable rate to buy their enterprises. Finally, while such laws and funding mechanisms in aid of co-ops are being developed, government support would include organizing a massive public discussion and debate over the issue of a social transition to a democratically organized economy.

One likely consequence of such transitions would be a redefinition of politics as we know it now. Parties would likely reorganize along the lines of which workplace organizations they favored and which they opposed. Where once socialist parties represented opposition to capitalism, they have long since morphed into parties advocating a kinder, gentler private capitalism with a more or less admixture of state capitalism (that is, government regulation and state-owned and - operated enterprises). In the wake of the emergence of the new 21st-century socialism, the next phase of socialist organizing would include advocating for, and helping to build, an economy based on worker co-ops. Various center-left and center-right political formations — including some socialist parties or wings of socialist parties — would become explicitly what they always were implicitly: supporters of a capitalist economy. Capitalists would be the base and support for such parties, while worker co-ops would become the same for socialist parties. Politics would again engage on a profound, regular, and hopefully non-violent basis with the question of whether capitalism or socialism better served the public good. The meanings of words and labels like "capitalism" and "socialism" would themselves change as this new political landscape emerged.

Worker co-ops are socialism's new vision and goal. They criticize the inherited socialism of the past while adding something crucial to it: a concrete vision of what an alternative, more just, and humane society would look like. With the new focus on workplace democratization, socialists are in a good position to contest the 21st century's struggle among economic systems.

Conclusion

To understand socialism now entails grasping how and why it is changing from what it was in its first two centuries, 1800 to 2000. Those years saw socialism grow from small, early, tentative experiments into mature national political parties, reorganized societies, and important state administrations. From several regional and national initiatives, it matured into an international tradition of diverse interpretations of its post-capitalist visions. Socialism inspired and produced a remarkable theoretical outpouring that took the criticism of capitalism to many new levels of sophisticated analyses, produced new critical literatures across all the disciplines, and also generated original designs and blueprints for the possible socialisms of the future. So fast and furious was socialism's growth and spread that its empirical record of trials and errors, successes and failures, provoked repeated periods of intense self-examination and self-criticism. Of these, the greatest flowed from the demise of Eastern European socialism in the 1980s, the changes in China, capitalism's neoliberal resurgence, and then the great capitalist crash of 2008 and since.

So profound was the impact on socialism of these key events of the last 40 years, that self-criticism went back to the roots of the tradition with basic questions. Socialists came to understand that the early decades of any social system are always times of experiments to find how to adjust theories and practices — to change the system — so that it can successfully reproduce itself and grow. Capitalism's early decades show that process. Socialists discovered that their system's early experiences likewise taught valuable lessons to those who dared to ask the questions and produce the answers. One lesson learned was that socialism must shift its prioritized focus from macro- to micro-level. The centrality of issues of ownership of the means of production (private or state), and distribution of resources and products by means of markets versus state planning, must be lessened. Instead, socialists' concentrated attention should move toward issues of hierarchy versus democracy inside workplaces. Socialists today are divided in how they see, feel, and react to such changes in their tradition. Worker co-ops already represent a key institutional embodiment of socialism's shifting foci. Time and struggle will tell how and how far they will come to represent the new socialism of the 21st century.

There is no way to understand socialism without understanding the yearnings for something better than capitalism. Capitalism ceaselessly reproduced those yearnings throughout its history. Socialism is capitalism's shadow, capitalism's persistent critic. Intertwined, capitalism and socialism change each other until their clashes finally result in something new and different — a new system with its new self-critical shadow. Like a bear emerging from hibernation, socialism today emerges from capitalism's often vicious, repressive effort to kill its own shadow. Of course that effort failed. Failure is built into capitalism's contradictions. But a revived socialism's new opportunities leave open the question of how well socialists see them, embrace their implications, and rebuild social movements strong enough to realize those opportunities. It is a question of 21st-century socialism responding adequately to those human yearnings to do better. We hope this book helps fashion such a response.

About the Cover:

The Red Rose as a Symbol of Socialism

The cover has been created by artist Luis de la Cruz. Luis is a graduate of Occidental College and also works as a firefighter. He has been illustrating portraits, cartoons, comic books, and t-shirt designs for organizations and individuals since high school. You can see more of Luis's work at www.luisdelacruzstudio.com.

The color red used on this cover has been a symbol of socialism since the French Revolution of 1848. After the fall of the Paris Commune in 1871, German Chancellor Bismarck, fearing a similar revolutionary outbreak in Germany, passed anti-Socialist laws that banned the red socialist flag. Getting around these laws, socialists began wearing small pieces of red ribbon to subtly show their political leanings. When these too were banned, they began to wear red roses. Socialists were arrested and jailed for wearing both the ribbons and the roses, and the push back on this eventually brought one's right to wear a flower to court. A judge finally ruled that citizens had a right to wear any flower of any color they wished, but that when a group of citizens gathered wearing red roses together, this constituted a socialist symbol.

The symbol of the red rose spread across Europe and to the US as socialists were exiled from France and Germany. By 1910, it was generally recognized as a symbol of socialism. Today, the red rose in a fist is the symbol of Socialist International (a worldwide organization of political parties), and the French Socialist Party. The red rose is also the symbol of the British Labour Party.

Thus, the red rose was an obvious choice for the cover of
Understanding Socialism. We chose to show multiple roses as a
demonstration of the growth and spread of socialism. Leaving
romanticism aside, our roses are straight, tall, proud, and strong.
The roses in the back are of a more faded opacity compared to the
front in order to show a passing of older versions of socialism and
the strength and rebirth of the new.

Bread and Roses

As we come marching, marching, in the beauty of the day,
A million darkened kitchens, a thousand mill-lofts gray
Are touched with all the radiance that a sudden sun discloses,
For the people hear us singing, "Bread and Roses, Bread and Roses."

As we come marching, marching, we battle, too, for men—
For they are women's children and we mother them again.
Our days shall not be sweated from birth until life closes—
Hearts starve as well as bodies: Give us Bread, but give us Roses.

As we come marching, marching, unnumbered women dead
Go crying through our singing their ancient song of Bread;
Small art and love and beauty their trudging spirits knew—
Yes, it is Bread we fight for—but we fight for Roses, too.

As we come marching, marching, we bring the Greater Days—
The rising of the women means the rising of the race.
No more the drudge and idler—ten that toil where one reposes—
But a sharing of life's glories: Bread and Roses, Bread and Roses.

Poem by James Oppenheim, published 1911.
Popularized in music by Mimi Fariña, Judy Collins, and Joan Baez.

About the Author

Richard D. Wolff is Professor of Economics Emeritus, University of Massachusetts, Amherst where he taught economics from 1973 to 2008. Earlier he taught economics at Yale University and at the City College of the City University of New York. Wolff was also a regular lecturer at the Brecht Forum in New York City. Professor Wolff was also among the founders in 1988 of the new academic association, Association of Economic and Social Analysis (AESA), and its quarterly journal Rethinking Marxism. He is currently a Visiting Professor in the Graduate Program in International Affairs of the New School University in New York City.

Professor Wolff is also the host of *Economic Update with Richard D. Wolff* which is produced and curated by his founding organization, Democracy at Work. His previous book with Democracy at Work was *Understanding Marxism* which was published in January of 2019.

Learn more: **www.rdwolff.com**

About the Editors

Liz Phillips is the Communications Director for Democracy at Work and has been on staff since early 2018. For the 2 years prior, she was a volunteer co-leader of a d@w Study Group in Los Angeles where she focused on content production and outreach. She obtained her BFA in Technical Theatre and Stage Management from the College of Santa Fe and in her subsequent 10 years of experience in entertainment (theater, dance, concerts, film, and advertising) she held mostly management / project leadership or creative / story-telling positions. She is thrilled to now put these skills to work advocating for the world she would like to see, increasing economic (and thus political) democracy for all through the proliferation of worker cooperatives.

Maria Carnemolla is the Media Director for Democracy at Work and has been on staff since 2013. She obtained her MS in Management from The College of St. Elizabeth in New Jersey. She has over 20 years of leadership experience working in higher education and nonprofit organizations. Her passion and enthusiasm for Leftism began at a young age and continues to this day. She has served as a member of the Board of Directors of the Left Forum and is also active in her community and children's schools. Maria is dedicated to working on moving to a more democratic economic system, one that puts people before profits.

About Democracy at Work

Democracy at Work is a non-profit 501(c)3 that produces media and live events. Based on the book *Democracy at Work: A Cure for Capitalism* by Richard D. Wolff, our work analyzes capitalism critically as a systemic problem and advocates for democratizing workplaces as part of a systemic solution. We seek a stronger, fuller democracy – in our politics and culture as well as in our economy – based on workers' equal collaboration and shared leadership inside enterprises and throughout society.

Democracy at Work produces the show *Economic Update with Richard D. Wolff* and *Global Capitalism Live Economic Update,* as well as the podcasts *David Harvey's Anti-Capitalist Chronicles*, *Capitalism Hits Home* with Dr. Harriet Fraad, and *All Things Co-op.*

Each of these is a collaborative effort, and are brought to you by the hard work and dedication of a small team of workers. To keep costs low, we work via a digital office and rely on donated time from Prof. Wolff as well as other volunteer contributors, like Prof. David Harvey and Dr. Harriet Fraad. We are a 501(c)3 but operate internally as a cooperative to better embody the ideals we believe are a critical part of effective system change.

Learn more: **www.democracyatwork.info**

Further Reading

- Samir Amin, *Eurocentrism,* Monthly Review Press; 2nd ed. Edition, 2010.
- Samir Amin, *Unequal Development,* Monthly Review Press; First Pr. Thus edition, 1976.
- Ian Angus, *A Redder Shade of Green: Intersections of Science and Socialism,* Monthly Review Press, 2017.
- David Bakhurst, *Consciousness and Revolution in Soviet Philosophy,* Cambridge University Press, 1991.
- Joseph Buttigieg, Translator and Editor, *Antonio Gramsci: Prison Notebooks, Vol. 1,* Columbia University Press, 1992.
- Amilcar Cabral, *Unity and Struggle: Selected Speeches and Writings,* Unisa Press; 2 edition, 2008.
- Christopher Caudwell, *Culture as Politics*, Monthly Review Press, 2018.
- Maurice Dobb, *On Economic Theory and Socialism,* Routledge Kegan & Paul, 2012.
- Albert Einstein, *Why Socialism?*, Monthly Review, 1949.
- Friedrich Engels, *Socialism: Utopian and Scientific,* International Publishers, 1935.
- Francis Fukuyama, *The End of History and the Last Man,* Free Press, 1992.
- Frances Goldin, *Imagine: Living in a Socialist USA,* Harper Perennial, 2014.
- Stuart Hall, *Selected Political Writings*, Duke University Press Books, 2017.
- C.L.R. James, *Black Jacobins,* Vintage; 2 edition, 1989.
- C.L.R. James, *At the Rendezvous of History,* Allison & Busby, 1984.
- Michael A. Lebowitz, *The Socialist Imperative: From Gotha to Now*, Monthly Review Press, 2015.
- Michael A. Lebowitz, *The Contradictions of Real Socialism,* Monthly Review Press, 2012.

- Minqi Li, *China and the Twenty-first-Century Crisis,* Pluto Press, 2015.
- Georg Lukacs, *Lenin: A Study on the Unity of his Thought,* Verso; 2 edition, 2009.
- Fritz Pappenheim, *The Alienation of Modern Man*, Monthly Review Press, 2010.
- Vincent Kelly Pollard, *State Capitalism, Contentious Politics and Large-Scale Social Change,* Haymarket Books, 2012.
- Brian Pollitt, Editor. *The Development of Socialist Economic Thought,* Lawrence & Wishart Ltd, 2008.
- Peter Ranis, *Cooperatives Confront Capitalism: Challenging the Neoliberal Economy,* Zed Books; Reprint edition, 2016.
- Stephen A. Resnick and Richard D. Wolff, *Class Theory and History: Capitalism and Communism in the USSR,* Routledge, 2002.
- Stephen A. Resnick and Richard D. Wolff, *Knowledge and Class,* University of Chicago Press, 1989.
- Antonio A. Santucci, *Antonio Gramsci,* Monthly Review Press; 1st edition, 2010.
- Nathan Schneider, *Everything for Everyone: The Radical Tradition That Is Shaping the Next Economy,* Bold Type Books; 1 edition, 2018.
- Bryan S. Turner, *Marx and the End of Orientalism,* Routledge; 1 edition, 2014.
- Richard D. Wolff, *Contending Economic Theories: Neoclassical, Keynesian, and Marxian,* MIT Press, 2012.
- Richard D. Wolff, *Democracy at Work: A Cure for Capitalism,* Haymarket Books, 2012.
- Richard D. Wolff, *Understanding Marxism*, Democracy at Work, 2019.